Jake Perry is a cricket writer and podcaster specialising in the Scottish game. He has written for *The Scotsman*, *All Out Cricket* and ESPNcricinfo and is a regular contributor to the websites of Cricket Scotland, Emerging Cricket and CRICKETher.

The Secret Game

Tales of Scottish Cricket

Jake Perry

Chequered Flag
PUBLISHING

First published in the UK by Chequered Flag Publishing 2020
3 Sparkham Close, Shrewsbury, SY3 6BX
www.chequeredflagpublishing.co.uk

Copyright © Jake Perry 2020
The moral right of the author has been asserted

All rights reserved
This book is sold subject to the condition that it may not, by way of trade or otherwise, be lent, resold, hired out or otherwise circulated without the publisher's prior consent in any form of binding or cover other than that in which it is published and without a similar condition including this condition being imposed on the subsequent purchaser

A CIP record for this book is available from the British Library

Printed in the EU by Print Group Sp. z o.o.

ISBN 978-1-9997774-6-3

To Susan, Emma, Douglas
and all who love Scottish cricket.

Contents

	Introduction	1
1.	Twenty-Two of Kelso	8
2.	Carlton and the Champion	22
3.	The Indomitable Carrick	35
4.	The Greatest Scot	44
5.	Shadows on the Esk	52
6.	Highland Games	62
7.	On the Promise of the Fruit	72
8.	English Captain, Scottish Heart	81
9.	From the Ashes	92
10.	Memories of Manjrekar	105
11.	The History Boys	116
12.	The Captain and the Goalie	125
13.	Pushing the Boundaries	138
14.	The Generation Game	156
	Notes	169
	Bibliography	173
	Acknowledgements	176
	Index	178

Introduction: A Hidden Heritage

On the afternoon of Sunday 10 June 2018, the best-kept secret in British sport was finally revealed.

Scotland's first ever win on the cricket field over England redefined not only the rivalry between the two nations – a deal of thinking again was no doubt taking place as the ICC's number one ranked team journeyed homeward – but the place of the game within the wider narrative of Scottish sport as well. For a few heady days cricket took centre stage as the country acknowledged the magnitude of what had been achieved in a sport of which many knew little. In a land fiercely proud of its golf but where football has always ruled, what had seemed that most unlikely of concepts – cricket in Scotland – was finally on the map.

The irony, of course, was that it always had been. Cricket has been part of the Scottish sporting landscape for well over two hundred years. From its introduction in the mid-eighteenth century and spread through migrant workers and the English-educated sons of the landed gentry, the game grew to become the foremost sport of the Scottish summer. Not only does it remain so today, but with over 150 clubs presently affiliated to Cricket Scotland as well as, by latest reckoning, more than 17,000 active participants, its health has seldom been better.

That the Scottish game has lived so much of its life under the radar of public consciousness, then, is as strange as it is difficult to explain. Although its numbers through the years have naturally ebbed and flowed, club cricket has never lost its intrinsic popularity; when it comes to the sport finding a place in the mainstream, however, there have always been others ready to muscle past it in the queue.

Writing in *'Play!'*, his 1946 memoir-cum-history of Edinburgh's Carlton Cricket Club, Norman L. Stevenson elaborated further on what was, even then, something of a forgotten existence.

'The collecting of the earliest playing records of the Carlton Cricket Club has proved difficult,' he sighed. 'The original members can no longer be consulted; the old scorebooks have long since disappeared. Even the ransacking of contemporary newspaper files furnishes information which is tantalisingly incomplete, for, during the first decade of the club's existence [the 1860s], cricket

INTRODUCTION

reports were often omitted from the "Sporting Annotations" of the day.

'There was at that time no Association football and, except among the boys of one or two Edinburgh schools, no rugby football. But there was plenty of golf, and the money matches of such old stalwarts of the cleek and gutty as Tom Morris, Tom Morris Jun., the Parks of Musselburgh, and "Old Crawford" ... were regularly and fully reported in the Press. Hunting news and racing results were never omitted. Special accounts were printed of the big shooting contests at Wimbledon. The killing of every large salmon was faithfully recorded. But, for many years, cricket, though it had long been firmly established as Scotland's most popular summer pastime, was the Cinderella of games so far as the Press was concerned.'[1]

The hunting and fishing reports may be gone, but the Cinderella tag has to a large extent remained.

Cricket, though, has been far from alone in its quest for greater exposure.

'The main factor facing virtually every sport in Scotland today is the obsession that the nation has with football and the belief that football is a Scottish sport and that Scotland is a football nation,' Malcolm Cannon, former Chief Executive of Cricket Scotland, told me. 'Whether that is true or not, it is the reality and there is little that can be done to change it.

'The situation that has been created as a result, however, is that there is very little room for anything else. I don't think that cricket is uniquely under-reported, but we certainly don't get the same amount of column inches that, for instance, rugby union or, on a good day, golf or tennis get. That's where the line is drawn, and anything below that, be it swimming or basketball or volleyball or sailing or whatever, just doesn't get the same level of coverage.

'It is nothing to do with participant numbers – look at athletics, for example, where there are huge numbers of people taking part – it's to do with sexiness. And, sadly, when it comes to that, nothing can compete with football in the eyes of the media.'

It is an issue which is hardly unique to Scotland, of course. The decline in the profile of English cricket has contrasted sharply with the ever-upward trajectory of football's Premier League, while the savvy marketing of American sport has brought a glamorous new challenge for hearts and minds from across the Atlantic. A 2016 survey of seven- to fifteen-year-olds found that only a third could correctly identify a photograph of then-England captain Alastair Cook; a majority, however, named American wrestler John Cena, one of the glitzy new breed of sports stars who have arrived to stake a claim on the ground once occupied by Compton, Trueman, Botham and the rest.

Scottish cricket, though, has had to deal with an additional phenomenon all of its own. Despite the debts owed by both football and rugby union to developments which took place south of the border, the singling-out of cricket as an 'English' game – which must, therefore, be somehow 'anti-Scottish' – presents a real, if absurd, challenge.

'There is a slice of Scotch opinion that views the game as some kind of colonial imposition and you can rely upon the chippier brand of nationalist to complain there's too much cricket on the television,' wrote Alex Massie. 'Not content with disliking the game themselves, they seem appalled that anyone else should like it.

'This is narrow-minded nonsense, of course, and an ignorance based upon discreditable presumptions about race and class. To hear some people talk, you'd think cricket is a game whose appeal in Scotland is restricted to aristocratic Quislings. I must say that this would surely come as news to folk in bastions of "elitist" privilege such as Greenock, Stenhousemuir, Coatbridge or Paisley, to say nothing of Aberdeenshire or the Borders. Anyone who actually has any experience of cricket in Scotland knows that cricket is a classless game.'[2]

While Massie concedes that there are plenty of other proud nationalists who are avid followers of the sport, his central point remains. In communities up and down the country, the suggestion that cricket is a pastime for the privileged few is simply not recognised, and doubters need not look far on a Saturday afternoon for proof of it.

Or, indeed, too hard at the history books. On 1 August 1903, for example, 10,000 spectators turned up at Perth's North Inch for the second day of the derby between Perthshire and Forfarshire – several being injured when a grandstand containing four hundred of them collapsed – while a similar number paid their money at Mannofield to watch Donald Bradman's last innings on British soil in 1948.[3]

Passions could run high. Richard Young tells of a dispute between the players of Thistle and Albion Cricket Clubs on Glasgow Green in 1832 which escalated into a mass brawl amongst the crowd.[4] A dubious umpiring decision was the cause; the authorities having to deal with its aftermath were unlikely to have found too much evidence of pseudo-upper-class reserve.

None of which is to imply that the notion of Scotland's 'classless game' has extended to a lack of quality on the field, of course. The country has produced more than its share of first-class cricketers, several of whom have gone on to grace the Test arena. Edinburgh-born Tom Campbell, for example, a 'light-hitting wicketkeeper' in Massie's wry assessment, played five Tests for South Africa between 1909 and 1912, while Archie Jackson, born in Rutherglen in 1909, was surely the 'greatest of Scottish and saddest of all Australian cricketers'.[5]

A number of others played Test cricket for England. Prominent amongst them is Mike Denness, a stylish batsman whose reign as England captain was overshadowed by the rival ambitions of teammate Geoffrey Boycott. The tension between them played a significant part in the Scot's ultimate downfall, but not before he had underlined his worth with back-to-back innings of 188 and 181 against Australia and New Zealand in 1975. Whatever the lasting impression of his captaincy may be, a Test average of a whisker below 40 – higher than those of Michael Atherton, Mike Gatting and Nasser Hussain, for example – combined with more than 25,000 first-class runs, says all that needs to be said about Denness as a cricketer.

Scotland has also welcomed a wealth of overseas talent to its shores, with Rohan Kanhai, Abdul Qadir, Gordon Greenidge, Desmond Haynes, Kim Hughes, Justin Langer, Adam Gilchrist, Sikandar Raza, Azhar Ali and Chris Martin just a few of those to have played club cricket in the Scottish leagues. Two of the finest bowlers in the international women's game, New Zealand's Leigh Kasperek and England's Kirstie Gordon, began their respective careers at Carlton and Huntly Cricket Clubs, too, and although both had to take the difficult decision to pursue opportunities away from their homeland, neither has forgotten their roots. Once a Scot, always a Scot, whatever the badge on the jersey.

All of which has brought me here. The history of cricket in Scotland is of a richness and antiquity to compare with that of any other country in the world, and my aim has been to capture something of that heritage: of its people and places, its clubs and their stories. Through contemporary sources and, wherever possible, the words of those who were there, I have sought to shine a light onto just a few of the tales of Scottish cricket, many of which are appearing in print for the first time. There are plenty of others waiting to be told; what follows is but a selection of them.

Scottish cricket has hidden in plain sight for too many years. If *The Secret Game* can contribute just a little in bringing it to the attention it deserves, I will be very happy.

I

TWENTY-TWO OF KELSO

Watching over Eros at the heart of Piccadilly Circus is all that is left of a sporting institution.

For well over a century the name of Lillywhites was synonymous with quality and service, its London store a place of pilgrimage for amateur and professional sportsmen alike. From its earliest days supplying cricket bats and cigars – essential tools for the gentlemen of the day – through to the move into the majestic Regent Street building it still occupies, the acquisition and subsequent transformation of Lillywhites into yet another branch of the megastore which so dominates sports retail in the twenty-first century has been a particularly sad chapter in the story of Britain's declining high street.

Up on the wall outside, though, is one last reminder of its past.

There, etched in gold, is the image of a batsman. Top-hatted, gloveless, bat respectfully straight as he takes his stance, the symbols of a long-lost age of English cricket hang heavy in the air – of gentlemen, players and halcyon days on the village green.

It is a tribute to both the founders of the company and the sport at which they excelled. From round-arm pioneer William to his sons John and Fred and nephew James, the Lillywhite family played a pivotal role in the development of cricket in England through the nineteenth century.* But while the reality behind the portrait has a harder edge than the rose-tinted vision it inspires, the story of the team in which John Lillywhite played uncovers a connection to the oldest club in Scotland, too.

Established in 1821,† Kelso Cricket Club has a history which predates the formation of Sussex, the first of

---

* William's eldest son, often referred to as James Snr to differentiate him from his more famous cousin, was also a first-class cricketer. He was employed by Glasgow cricket club Clydesdale as their professional in the 1850s but, perhaps most significantly in the wider development of Scottish sport, provided the committee of the newly formed Queen's Park Football Club with their first copy of football's 'Rules of the Field' in August 1867 (Richard S. Young, *As the Willow Vanishes*, 2014, p.95).

† Although 1821 is widely accepted as the date of Kelso's foundation, it is possible that the club was, in fact, formed the year before. Kelso's Minutes Book of 1821-1830 (held in the Scottish Borders Archive and Local History Centre in St. Mary's, Selkirk) provides the earliest surviving evidence of the activities of the club, but, intriguingly, describes itself as covering Kelso's 'Second Session'. The implied earlier volume has been lost, but it may well be that Scotland's oldest club played its first matches in 1820 (David Potter, *The Encyclopaedia of Scottish Cricket*, 1999, pp.112-114).

the English county teams, by eighteen years. Based in the town's Shedden Park since 1851, the club was a founder member of the historic Border League, a competition in which it continued to play until its move into the Scottish National League and, in due course, to the divisions of the East of Scotland Cricket Association.

Proof that cricket flourished in the Borders long before it was formally organised, however, is found within the pages of a precious volume from the Kelso archive. Beginning with the visit of Berwick on 7 August 1850, the hand-written scorebook offers a unique insight into the cricket played in the town as it lived through one of the most important phases in the development of the game. Club cricket was on the rise, and with regular matches against teams from the north of England and Edinburgh as well as local rivals Melrose, Hawick and Wilton, Selkirk, Galashiels and Dunse – later to become Manderston – the cricketers of Kelso were clearly reaping the benefits.

That they were playing a somewhat different game to the one we know today, however, is also very apparent. The improved bats and shorter boundaries of more recent years may have tilted the balance of power towards the batsman, but the rough, weather-exposed pitches of the nineteenth century ensured that it was the Victorian era which would be the red-letter time to be a bowler.

Batting was a risky business in those early days. The absence of a sightscreen meant that the ball was easily lost in the background and, with protective gear primitive and pitches unpredictable, most batsmen chose to play off the back foot for their own safety, making them easy pickings for skilful bowlers. Physical demands were also high, as on grounds lacking natural boundaries each scoring shot had to be run out in full, resulting in many a batsman losing his wicket to sheer fatigue. All in all, it is little wonder that a career batting average in double figures was considered commendable.

The first entry in the scorebook provides a typical illustration, as having taken twenty overs* to dismiss Berwick for 31, Kelso managed only 23 in reply. Even a small advantage was significant, of course, and the visitors first strengthened it with the bat then drove it home with the ball. Berwick's second innings total of 52 left Kelso requiring 61, a target which proved well beyond them as they were bowled out for 30 to lose by a similar margin. Forty wickets had fallen for a combined total of 136 runs – all, it should be added, in the space of a single afternoon.

Recorded alongside the serious business of inter-club cricket is the quirky, too. 'Married' met 'Single' in a two-innings game on 10 August 1860 – 'Married' triumphing by 12 runs in a fixture which was popular in Georgian and early Victorian Britain – while the *Kelso Chronicle* reported on a match played between 'two Elevens of Kelso Cricket Club' at Kelso Race Course 'for strawberries, to be paid [for] by the losing side.'

The victors 'met in the Queen's Head Inn ... and partook of the fruit, with the requisite adjuncts, and spent the evening in a social and agreeable manner,' the piece continues.

'The playing of this club is carried on with great keenness and spirit,' it concludes. 'Many of the members have

---

* Each over consisted of four balls, as was the norm until the introduction of five-ball overs in 1889. The familiar six-ball over did not appear until the beginning of the twentieth century.

already attained a proficiency which would not discredit those of a much longer established club.'[1]

The irony of his last sentence appears to have passed our anonymous correspondent by.

Dicey pitches and novelty games were not the only things to differentiate Victorian cricket from its modern-day equivalent, however. In the nineteenth century, 'odds' matches, which pitted a particularly strong eleven against a team of inflated numbers, were another familiar part of the sporting landscape. Kelso played a representative Sixteen of the Borders in September 1858, for example, in a game which featured twelve second-innings wickets for long-serving Kelso professional Reynolds in his team's seven-wicket victory at Shedden Park.

There are other such encounters, though, which particularly catch the eye.

More than eighty years before Abe Saperstein revolutionised the game of basketball with the launch of the Harlem Globetrotters, another band of players-for-hire was hitting the road for the first time. This group of hand-picked professionals, taking advantage of the railway network's rapid expansion and the growing demand to see top-class cricket, began to tour the country to take on local sides keen to test themselves against the very best that the English game had to offer.

The brainchild of William Clarke – cricketer, entrepreneur and the original owner of Trent Bridge – the All-England Eleven played its first match at the back end of the 1846 season. In their dapper uniforms of red-spotted white shirts, white trousers, neckerchiefs and stylish top hats, the Eleven captured the imagination of a whole new audience, and fans came from far and wide to see such big-name players as Nicholas Felix, Fuller Pilch and Alfred Mynn show off their skills.

Fairs and other side attractions added a little Victorian-style razzmatazz to the event for the enthusiastic crowds of paying public. For Clarke, his players and any local impresarios with a little imagination, there was money to be made.*

The All-England Eleven made its first appearance north of the border in 1849 against a Scotland Twenty-Two at Edinburgh's Spark's Ground.† Despite a heavy defeat for the hosts the public success of the fixture was considerable, and after a return visit the following year and two games in 1851, the Eleven began its 1852 schedule with a fifth trip to the capital.

In a match beginning on 10 May, the Twenty-Two initially held its own, finishing the first innings only four runs in deficit despite Clarke's slow under-arm leg-spin accounting for twelve Scottish wickets at a cost of only 46. The second was decisive, though, as Scotland's 54 in reply to All-England's 138 confirmed another hefty loss, this time by an 88-run margin.

Six of that Scotland side were to get another chance against the professionals in the autumn, however, as on 20

---

* Clarke typically charged local promoters a fee of around £70 for the hire of his team, plus a share of the gate revenues and, as writer James Pycroft put it, 'much hospitality' (Richard Tomlinson, *Amazing Grace*, 2015, p.8).

† Although described as 'Scotland', the team which played the All-England Eleven was not representative in the sense of the term as we understand it today. The early Scotland Twenty-Twos were organised on an ad hoc basis for the specific occasion, combining amateurs – often including members of the titled gentry – with professionals. It was not until 1865 that Scotland's first recognised 'capped' game took place.

September they lined up as part of a Twenty-Two of Kelso for the beginning of a three-day game at Shedden Park.*

Such an arrangement was far from unusual. Rather than being made up of purely home-grown talent, the local twenty-twos often included a number of guests who had been brought in for the occasion from elsewhere, and Kelso's team was typical in featuring several who had little or no previous connection to the town.

Some came up from England, bringing with them a healthy pedigree in first-class cricket. Cambridgeshire-born professional Alfred 'Ducky' Diver, for example, would go on to make several appearances for the All-England Eleven himself, while round-arm medium-pacer Francis Tinley's nineteen-match record of sixty-five wickets at 9.34, mostly for his native Nottinghamshire, would be crowned by a best of six for 29 at The Oval ten months later. With Viscount Dupplin, the President of Marylebone Cricket Club (MCC), and Lord Henry Paget, the future Marquess of Anglesey, arriving in the Borders, too, it was an eclectic mix of gentlemen and players which came together under the banner of the home team.

The game would prove to be a nip-and-tuck encounter with an exciting finish. After Tinley's seven for 25 had limited the visitors to 59, Clarke put his team on top with eleven for 27 as the Twenty-Two was bowled out for only 45 in reply. The pendulum swung again, however, as Tinley took a further seven for 11 to skittle the professionals

---

* Although arranged as a three-day game, Clarke was persuaded to stay on for a fourth in order to finish it. 'This is the only four-days' match I ever took part in in the United Kingdom,' wrote All-England's William Caffyn (*Seventy-One Not Out*, 1899, p.75).

for just 27. It had been a game for the bowlers again, but Kelso's batsmen now had a chance to make their mark. Requiring 41 for a famous win, the home side inched towards its target. Tinley, batting at nine, fought his way to 11, the only second innings batsman on either side to reach double figures, but with a steady stream of wickets falling around him the task was to ultimately prove too great. His dismissal, caught and bowled by the ubiquitous Clarke, extinguished any remaining hope of an upset as Kelso's 79-over vigil was ended a mere eight runs short of the finishing line.

It was, wrote Borders historian William Anderson, a match which 'owed much to the elementary state of the wicket in [those] days.'[2] Not that Clarke was complaining. His thirty-nine second innings overs, twenty-nine of which were maidens, had brought him a memorable haul of fourteen for 14.

Although William Clarke was, to use that beautifully understated euphemism, a 'difficult' man off the field, there is no doubting his prowess on it. While many of his contemporaries switched to bowling in the new round-arm style as it gained in popularity, Clarke continued to develop and refine his under-arm technique to the point where it became all but unplayable. Delivering the ball with a whipping action and curving flight, his deliveries found vicious turn off the pitch, and in taking five wickets in an innings eighty-two times and ten wickets in a match on a further twenty-five occasions the Nottinghamshire captain should rightly be remembered as one of the greatest spin bowlers to have played the game. The conditions of the day may have been to his advantage, but

Clarke's record of 795 wickets at 9.99, gathered from the 143 appearances he made in his forty-one years of first-class cricket, speaks for itself.

His personality, however, ensured that trouble was never far away, and by the time All-England arrived in Kelso a schism had already split its ranks. Although Clarke had always been careful to ensure that his players received better wages than those paid by either the counties or MCC, he had been less than discreet when it came to flaunting the fortune he had made for himself, and with no sign of a pay rise on the cards, a group of players led by John Wisden and James 'Jemmy' Dean decided to break away to form an organisation of their own, the pointedly-named United All-England Eleven, midway through the summer of 1852.

The newcomers, much to Clarke's disgust, proved to be similarly popular as they, too, began their travels. With local promoters recouping the costs of hiring the team through ticket sales, Wisden and Dean replicated their erstwhile employer's business model, and over the next few seasons fixtures were arranged with teams from all around the country, including many of the All-England Eleven's long-standing opponents.*

The United All-England Eleven visited Scotland for the first time in September 1854 to play back-to-back games against representative twenty-twos in Edinburgh and Glasgow. Two more comprehensive defeats for the hosts duly followed, but the next year was to finally bring

---

* William Clarke would have nothing to do with the new team, but after his death in 1856 the two professional elevens played regularly against each other, instigating a rivalry which grew to become the most eagerly anticipated encounter of the English summer.

some home success. Nine wickets from slow under-armer Edward Drake took the Scots to their first-ever win over the professionals in September 1855, before round-arm medium-pacer Charles Brampton took thirteen in the match to see Scotland triumph again on the English team's next visit north in 1857.

On 28 September, two days after their second defeat on Scottish soil, United All-England began a three-day match against another Twenty-Two of Kelso. As well as Dean and Wisden – seven years before he published the first edition of his eponymous *Cricketer's Almanack* – all-rounder William Caffyn, wicketkeeper Tom Lockyer and fast round-arm bowler James Grundy were amongst the all-star line-up which took to the field.

Also at Shedden Park that day was the thirty-year-old John Lillywhite. In addition to his appearances for United All-England, William's eldest son played first-class cricket for Sussex, Middlesex and MCC, taking 223 wickets at an average of 11.56. With two centuries and thirteen fifties to his name too, the Hove-born all-rounder was very much a player in the family tradition.

It was Caffyn who excelled in Kelso, though, as in the first innings he posted what turned out to be the highest score of the game. His 37 set the Eleven on its way to a total of 112, and although the Kelso bowlers gave a good account of themselves, Brampton taking five for 48 and Sewell four for 27, history told the hosts that the outcome of the match was going to rest on their success – or otherwise – with the bat.

Sadly for the Borderers it was to prove to be the latter. Only two Kelso batsmen made it into double figures as their side limped to 72, and despite the Eleven totalling only 71 themselves in their second innings, an outstanding performance from John Wisden put the final seal onto their victory.

Bowling unchanged in partnership with Caffyn for 54.1 overs, the Sussex bowler took fifteen for 20 as the Twenty-Two was dismissed for 52. Whether it was with his medium-pace round-arm or slow under-arm – Wisden bowled either – the Kelso batsmen, with a total of seventeen ducks between them over the course of the match, had clearly found him too much to handle.

In 1859, five members of that United All-England side – Wisden, Caffyn, Lillywhite, Lockyer and Grundy – joined the twelve-man party which set sail for North America on the first ever overseas tour by an English side.* A combination of players from the All-England and United All-England Elevens and captained by George Parr, stalwart of William Clarke's original team, the tourists played five matches against local twenty-twos together with a further three eleven-a-side exhibition games as they looked to further the interest being shown in cricket in the place where it seemed most likely to flourish in the future.†

---

* Cricketing entrepreneur Fred Lillywhite also travelled to North America. Although never a player of particular note himself, William's third son was the driving force behind the family business and the editor of the *Guide to Cricketers*, the most significant cricketing publication before *Wisden Cricketers' Almanack*. Fred was also well known for his pitchside publishing operation, facilitated via a portable printing press in his scoring tent, which would often feature in the United All-England Eleven's advertising as they toured the country. From 1867 – the year after Fred's death – the Guide was incorporated into James Lillywhite's *Cricketers' Companion*.

† The onset of the American Civil War eighteen months later ensured that the success of Parr's tour could not be properly capitalised upon. Enthusiasm for cricket gradually faded during the war years as the troops on both sides adopted the embryonic game of baseball, and when English teams resumed tours to North America in

Back at home, meanwhile, the travelling elevens continued to ply their trade, and on 22 September, two days before Parr's team played its first match in Montreal, Kelso welcomed United All-England back to the Borders. With so many big names away in North America it was a very different line-up to the one which had triumphed two years before, but with Nottinghamshire's Richard Daft, Surrey's George Griffith and the formidable Jemmy Dean still in its ranks, the task facing the hosts was hardly less daunting.

Again, though, the Borderers could call on some notable players of their own. George Dickins, a Major in the 21st Fusiliers and first-class cricketer for Kent, had a history against the professional elevens which stretched back to Scotland's first game against All-England in 1849. A left-handed batsman and slow right-arm lob-bowler, the Major played a significant role in the development of Borders cricket after his move to the area from the south of England.

Dickins played against the All-England and United All-England Elevens a total of fifteen times in the years between 1849 and 1864. He clearly caught the eye of his opponents, too, and was rewarded with an appearance alongside Lillywhite, Wisden and company in United All-England's game against Stockton and Middlesbrough in September 1863. But it was Kelso which was closest to his heart, and through the 1860s and '70s the enthusiasm and cricketing ability of Dickins was central to his

---

1868, they now had both apathy and a serious rival to contend with. Scott Reeves provides a comprehensive account of the story in his excellent book, *The Champion Band* (2014).

adoptive town fielding one of the best teams in southern Scotland.*

On the other side of the country, meanwhile, Colonel David Carrick Robert Carrick-Buchanan would soon fulfil a similar role as a founder of West of Scotland Cricket Club. He was also no stranger to Shedden Park, having been amongst those drafted in for Kelso's game against All-England in 1852, and he was again invited to strengthen the Borderers' ranks as they prepared for their third, and ultimately final, visit from a professional eleven.

The opening exchanges could hardly have been closer. After Lee's five wickets helped the Twenty-Two dismiss United All-England for 81, Jemmy Dean took eleven for 40 and Frederick Reynolds eight for 31 to bowl the hosts out for 82, a first innings lead of a single run.

The professionals moved ahead with Reynolds (18) joining George Anderson (31) and William Mortlock (25) in contributing the lion's share of their second innings total of 99, and with Kelso now requiring the same to win, the fate of the game rested, yet again, on the fourth innings.

Once more, though, it was not to be. Slow under-armer William Mudie took twelve for 29 as the Twenty-Two subsided to 45 all out, and with fellow lobber Reynolds collecting a further five wickets at a cost of only 12, the United All-England Eleven wrapped up its second victory over Kelso by a margin of more than fifty runs.

---

* George Dickins' two sons were also accomplished cricketers, with one of them, Ambrose, going on to represent Scotland against an England XI at Merchiston Castle on 23 May 1878. He made his fortune in banking after emigrating to Canada, where his own son played a leading role in the early development of the aviation industry.

As popular as they were, the days of the travelling elevens were already numbered. With the growth of the county game and the introduction of international cricket, the public demand so astutely judged by William Clarke nearly four decades before at last began to wane. Both the All-England and United All-England Elevens had disappeared altogether by 1880, three years after the inaugural Test match had been played between Australia and an England side captained by James Lillywhite, cousin of John. The times, and cricket, had moved on.

Yet Kelso Cricket Club can look back on an association with some of the most famous names in the history of the game. As the current generation of Kelso cricketers walks out onto Shedden Park today, they can do so in the knowledge that they are following in some of the most illustrious footsteps of all.

2

Carlton and the Champion

On 23 May 1872, five years before the historic first Test was played in Melbourne, England's future captain was taking to the field in Edinburgh. James Lillywhite was part of a new travelling team, and together with Harry Jupp, Henry Charlwood and James Southerton,[*] three more who would be adding the title of 'Test cricketer' to their CVs in Australia, he joined the United South of

---

[*] At 49 years and 119 days, Southerton is still the oldest player to have made a Test debut.

England Eleven* for the first of two early-season matches in Scotland.

Standing alongside him, though, was a man who already overshadowed them all.

More than a century on from his death, the world of cricket is still to see a more influential figure than WG Grace. Widely credited with the invention of modern batting technique, his remarkable achievements captured the imagination of the public in a way that only Bradman would come close to emulating.† 'Grace's towering presence, more than any other single factor, transformed cricket into the unrivalled spectator sport of summer,' wrote Geoffrey Moorhouse, 'first of all in England, subsequently in other lands spread widely across the world.'[1]

Just a glance at his story is enough to show why. The first-class summer of 1871, for example, saw Grace account for ten of the season's seventeen centuries as he racked up 2,739 runs at an average of 78.25, almost double that of Richard Daft, his nearest rival. On 10 August 1876 he became the first batsman to score a first-class triple century – eight days later he had become the first to score two – while in 1895 the month of May brought Grace both a thousand runs and his hundredth hundred

---

* The United South of England Eleven had been founded in the midst of a north-south split within professional cricket which centred on ill-feeling arisen between Nottinghamshire and Surrey. Established in November 1864 by Edgar Willsher and John Lillywhite, the United South was formed almost entirely from players who had previously played for the All-England and, particularly, United All-England Elevens. A rival United North of England Eleven was set up in 1869.

† In his book *Amazing Grace* (2015), Richard Tomlinson recounts the story of Henry Morton Stanley's arrival in Adelaide to begin a lecture tour in 1891. The celebrated explorer, waiting on deck to be formally greeted, was ignored by the onrushing group of well-wishers in their eagerness to shake the hand of WG at the start of his second Australian tour (p.x).

just a few weeks short of his forty-seventh birthday. Four years later, he was still opening the batting for England.

No wonder *Lillywhite's Companion* hailed him as the 'Champion Cricketer'. Surviving film of Grace suggests that he may not have been the most stylish batsman around, but it is hard to imagine anyone with a greater sense of panache.

Or, when it came to mastering the potentially lethal conditions of the day, a higher degree of skill. At Lord's on 15 June 1870, the day after Grace had added yet another century to his record, Nottinghamshire batsman George Summers was struck on the left cheekbone by a ball which reared up so sharply that MCC wicketkeeper William Yardley thought it must have hit a stone. Helped from the field and given a glass of brandy – 'the last thing,' as 'Plum' Warner observed, 'to do in the circumstances' – Summers spent the following day watching in the hot sun before catching his train back to the Midlands in the evening.[2] Seriously ill by the time he arrived, the twenty-five-year-old's condition progressively worsened until, four days after he received the blow, he finally succumbed to its effects. MCC, having paid for his tombstone, began efforts to improve the Lord's pitch; John Platts, the unfortunate bowler who had delivered the fateful ball, never bowled fast again.

William Gilbert Grace had been born into a family which combined a calling to the medical profession with an all-consuming addiction to cricket. His brother Edward, coroner for the Lower Division of Gloucestershire, once had a corpse put on ice so he could continue with his game, while WG himself, having begun his studies at the Bristol Medical School as a bachelor in 1868, did not get round to completing them until he was a married father of three a full eleven years later thanks to his commitments on the cricket field.

The year of his eventual graduation was a notable one for cricket in Scotland, too. The first incarnation of the Scottish Cricket Union was born and, although it would be only four years until financial pressure caused its disbandment, an important landmark in the future organisation of the sport had been reached.

Amongst the twenty-five original members of the SCU was a club which was already at the forefront of cricket in the nation's capital. Carlton Cricket Club had come a long way in the sixteen years since its foundation, and it was thanks to the ambition of its members that Scottish crowds were given their first chance to see the world's greatest cricketer for themselves.

Back in 1863, the gentlemen of Edinburgh's St Bernard's Literary and Debating Society had agreed to form a cricket club to provide a suitably wholesome activity to occupy their summer months. Taking its name from London's Conservative-dominated Carlton Club – 'the promotors being very Tory'[3] – and colours from the twin blues of Oxford and Cambridge, the new team joined the host of others already playing at Stockbridge Park and on the Meadows, the large public park in the centre of the city still well used by club cricketers today.*

Success came quickly, and by 1866 Carlton's financial position had improved to the point where a piece of pri-

---

* Norman Stevenson's *'Play!'* identifies a further thirty-eight clubs based on the Meadows or at Stockbridge Park at the same time (p.14).

vate land could be rented on the city's Grange Loan.* Its wickets were little better than the public ones that had been left behind, however, and so in 1869 the club moved again, to a plot known as Little Transylvania – 'a reference to trees and silviculture, rather than vampires' – on nearby St. Thomas Road.[4]

Still, though, the facilities left much to be desired. 'Doubtless the Carlton made the pitch as good as it was possible to make it,' reported the *Evening Courant* in its write up of a match between Carlton and Kelso that same year, 'but with all their labours it was very bad and the ball bumped frequently as high as the batsman's shoulders.'[5]

It would have been interesting to see what WG could have made of such a challenge, but Little Transylvania was not the venue Carlton had in mind for the visit of his team. Instead it was Craigmount Park, an 'excellent field' situated next to Carlton's present-day home on Grange Loan, which provided the setting for the Champion Cricketer's first appearance in Scotland.[6]

The decision to invite the United South had been taken at a meeting of the Carlton committee on 24 November 1871†. 'The Secretary mentioned that this meeting was called for the purposes of considering whether the United South of England Eleven should be brought down,' the minutes record. 'There being no counter-motion [the proposal] was unanimously agreed.

---

*   Initially shared with the Edinburgh Caledonian Cricket Club, the venue subsequently became known as 'Carlton Ground'.

†   The meeting also discussed a request that permission be granted to a recently formed 'Foot Ball Club' [sic] to play on Carlton's ground, noting that 'any overflow of money there might be in the Foot Ball Club's hands would be handed over to the funds of the Cricket Club'.

'The Chairman then proposed that a Committee should be formed to make up [a] list of Twenty-Two Gentlemen to play against [the] Eleven and manage sundry things that might crop up connected.'[7]

The committee's final list naturally included a healthy number from Carlton. GF Rayner, JB Richardson – a one- and two-mile running champion known locally as 'Carlton Dick' – and CH Hayman[*] were amongst those who joined their captain Dr Duncan McDonald, a lob-bowling all-rounder who 'worked sixteen hours a day and could [still] find the time to play cricket', at Craigmount Park for the start of the game.[8] With the Scots keen to show the Edinburgh public exactly what they were made of, hopes were high as visiting bowler James Southerton got the match underway.

For the hosts, however, the clatter of wickets soon revealed the full extent of the task which lay ahead. Edinburgh lost its top seven for a combined total of only 10, and although Joseph Cotterill began his innings with two sixes off Southerton, his departure soon after, caught and bowled by the Sussex slow round-armer for 14, marked the beginning of another run of single-figure scores for the beleaguered home team.

Batting at fifteen, W. Cunningham's 20 stands out on a card in which only he and Cotterill reached double figures, and in the end it was appropriate that it was Southerton, as catcher, and Lillywhite, as bowler, who combined to see him on his way. The two had bowled unchanged to dismiss the Gentlemen for 77, and as they left the field to

---

[*] Messrs. Rayner, Richardson and Hayman are always referred to by their initials in Carlton's records of the time and despite further enquiries, their first names remain elusive. The same can be said of any others so named in subsequent chapters.

the applause of the 3,000 spectators who had braved the 'somewhat uninviting' late spring weather, it was now up to the batsmen to build on their success.[9]

Shortly after the lunch interval, openers WG Grace and Harry Jupp strode to the middle to begin the visitors' reply. WG was quickly off the mark with a single, but having added only seven more he 'played forward too soon and was cleverly caught by JB Richardson.'[10] The Gentlemen had the wicket they wanted, and Carlton Dick had a story to tell his grandchildren.

As, soon after, would William St Clair Grant. Richard Humphrey, a dangerous batsman who would tour Australia with Grace the following year, scored only 1 before he was bowled by the talented nineteen-year-old. St Clair Grant would go on to play international rugby for Scotland;* with the South on 22 for two as stumps were drawn at the end of the day, however, he had put his cricket team into a very promising position.

Day two began in 'delightful weather' as Jupp and new batsman Fred Grace returned to the crease.[11] The threat of WG had been overcome – for now at least – but his twenty-one-year-old brother was a more than capable player in his own right.

Fred† – GF Grace – was a genuine all-rounder, combining powerful hitting and fast round-arm bowling with outstanding fielding and, when occasion demanded, wick-

---

* William St Clair Grant's son, also called William, played first-class cricket for Gloucestershire. A captain in the Cameroon Highlanders during World War One, he was awarded the Military Cross and the Croix de Guerre Belge shortly before his death in a Passchendaele field hospital on 26 September 1918 at the age of twenty-four.
† Fred and WG appeared for the United South as amateurs by virtue of the medical training which they were undertaking. Neither was unpaid, however – while the professionals received a flat fee of £5 per game, both were allowed to claim for

etkeeping. Said to be a more attractive but less patient bat than his older sibling, his 195-match first-class return of 6,906 runs, 329 wickets, 171 catches and three stumpings nevertheless point to a highly gifted young player.*

At Craigmount Park, however, Fred's contribution amounted to just 4 before he was caught, and after the solid but unspectacular Jupp – his nickname of 'Young Stonewaller' was well-earned – was run out by Crole for 14, the South lost its last few wickets cheaply. Henry Charlwood reached 19, but with the final six batsmen adding just 9 between them, the United South ended its first innings an awkward 17 runs behind.

The next was to effectively settle the game. The South restarted strongly as Edinburgh lost its top eight for a combined total of 20, while WG chipped in with the wicket of Alexander Duncan, caught by Fred for a single. By the time the Edinburgh man departed, however, a match-winning performance was already underway at the other end.

Twenty-year-old Joseph Cotterill's brief but belligerent knock on the first day had given a hint of what was to come. The Sussex-born medical student had recently

---

expenses which typically amounted to far more. 'Shamateurism' was a charge which would dog WG in particular throughout his career.

* Fred's story would ultimately be one of potential left unfulfilled by tragedy. In September 1880, along with his brothers WG and EM, he appeared against Australia at The Oval in what was later recognised as the first Test match to be played in England. The three enjoyed mixed fortunes – while WG had opened his international account with 152 and EM a respectable 36, Fred had got a pair, although he had provided a memorable moment under the gasometer by holding onto a steepling catch from George Bonnor which is said to have travelled 115 yards. During the match, however, he developed a cold which rapidly escalated to pneumonia, thanks in part to being caught in the rain while playing for the United South against Stroud the following week. Aged twenty-nine, the youngest of the Grace brothers died just two weeks after his England debut.

arrived in Edinburgh to take up a place at the city's University, and over the next few seasons his performances for Grange Cricket Club would establish him as one of Scotland's most reliable players.* 'Although not a very tall gentleman,' wrote Glasgow journalist David Drummond Bone, 'Dr Cotterill surprised all who saw him bat by his long reach, and his powerful forward drive from the offside, with the ball low down, was simply grand.'[12]

Re-entering the fray at Craigmount Park, Cotterill completely dominated the scoring, hitting Southerton for two sixes before going on to 'serve Lillywhite hotly in a variety of ways so that bowling changes had to be made'.[13] Exactly how 'hotly' can be judged from the end-of-day scorecard. Of Edinburgh's 99 for seven, Cotterill, having come in at nine, had contributed 83. It had been an extraordinary performance.

Two more sixes on the final morning took him to the cusp of a century and, although disappointment then followed as he was caught at long-on by Fred Grace, the Edinburgh batsman's free-scoring had put his side into an all but impregnable position. The South looked to bat out a draw, but once WG had departed for 17, caught once again by Richardson, only Charlwood (35) and Pooley (25) offered significant further resistance. William Laidlay sealed a 63-run win for Edinburgh with his fourth wicket of the innings as the United South was bowled out for 107.

James Southerton finished the match with twenty-seven for 115, but it was Cotterill's 95, with its 'five mighty hits out of the ground', which would be remembered.[14]

---

* Cotterill also played thirty-seven first-class matches for Sussex, for whom he scored 1708 runs at an average of 27.11.

'Mr [sic] McDonald, the captain of the Twenty-Two, in a few complimentary remarks, presented Cotterill with one of Cobbett's bats, furnished by King* for his fine display,' wrote an observer.[15] The Edinburgh public may not have seen a vintage performance from WG, but it had certainly got its money's worth.†

Three days after their defeat in the east of Scotland, the United South looked for a change of fortune in the west. In a match against a Twenty-Two of Glasgow arranged by the city's Caledonian Club, the presence of WG was again the major draw as, on 30 May, another large crowd gathered at the club's Holyrood Park ground.

As in the capital, though, they would have to wait while the hosts batted first. Opening the bowling for the South once more, the wily Southerton took eleven for 78, but in reaching 154 the Twenty-Two ended its first innings in a commanding position.

Their strength then turned to dominance as Clydesdale's Andrew McAllister and West of Scotland's Charles McInnes combined to dismiss the visitors for just 49 in reply. While McInnes removed the opening pair of Jupp (0) and Charlwood (6) as well as wicketkeeper Ted Pooley (6), McAllister's seven wickets ensured that his team would carry a lead of over a hundred into the second innings.

'[McAllister] was a grand bowler … known over the whole of Scotland,' wrote Bone. 'He had somewhat of a peculiar delivery, pretty high, with the ball coming off the

---

* As well as owning a sports shop on Edinburgh's Lothian Road, Percival King edited the *Scottish Cricketers' Annual*, an indispensable record of the game in the latter part of the nineteenth century.
† As, indeed, had Carlton. The organisers cleared a profit of over £100 on the three-day game, a tidy sum which went a long way towards keeping the club in a healthy financial position in the years that followed.

ground with a rattling good spin. Many opponents who met Mr McAllister's bowling for the first time were a good deal puzzled with it, and not unfrequently fell softly.'[16]

Bone highlights McAllister's performance against the United South as his best ever. It is fair to say, however, that not all were fully appreciative of it.

'The feature of the contest ... was the enthusiasm with which the spectators entered into the game and the eager way every run was watched and criticised,' he wrote. 'Many ... [who] had a burning desire to see the Champion bat, could almost have kicked Mr Lawrence Thomson* for catching him out in hitting his first ball from Mr McAllister.

'The drive was a good one to the off-side, and Mr Thomson was just leaving a friend at the ropes when he rushed in on seeing the ball coming towards him and collared it ... It was hinted – but what grounds there were for it Mr A. Watt, the deceased captain of the Caledonian, alone could tell us – that the said captain was so put about at the unlooked-for incident that he wished Mr Thomson had dropped the ball.'[17]

Watt may well have entertained the thought, but Bone dismisses out of hand the notion of him acting on it in a passage which carries a certain wry resonance today.

'In many varieties of sport where the lower animals are engaged,' he sniffed, 'some results are looked upon

---

* It appears that Bone has misremembered the name of the fielder as it was JG Stewart who took the catch to dismiss Grace in the first innings. The Caledonian Club's Lawrence Thomson was not playing that day, but, as it was his club which had organised the fixture, it is not unlikely that he was present at the ground. This, perhaps, explains the writer's mistake when recalling the incident more than twenty years later.

with suspicion as being "squared", but in cricket, above all games, "squaring" is impossible.

'What player can resist the noble impulse of making a good catch, even though he should lose money to his club by it? None that I have ever seen, and for that part of it, who has ever heard of a batsman deliberately allowing his wicket to go down?'[18]

In the event no skulduggery was required. As the South followed on[*] in front of a crowd which had swelled to around 7,000, WG Grace's first Scottish century at last rewarded the supporters with what they had come to see.

'It was fine to watch the quiet self-possession of the man as he met attacks of every sort his assailants could devise, and especially fine to witness the wonderful precision with which he could follow the course even of a shooting ball and quickly intercept it within six inches of the stumps,' wrote Bone. 'In the second innings, when he had it all his own way, and dashed right and left like another Samson, the sensation-loving crowd had a bellyful.'[19]

His innings of 112 gave the Eleven hope, but despite Southerton, Lillywhite and Fred Grace taking fifteen wickets between them as the Twenty-Two batted again, it had not been quite enough. After 75.2 overs the target of 92 was passed, confirming a six-wicket win for the hosts and a second defeat on Scottish soil for their renowned opponents.

WG Grace would make several more visits to Scotland in the years after 1872, not least to collect the LRCP[†] diploma from the University of Edinburgh which finally enabled him to qualify as a doctor. In 1877 he scored a

---

[*]   A deficit of 60 runs on first innings was the follow-on threshold at the time.
[†]   Licentiate of the Royal Colleges of Physicians

century for the United South at the city's Raeburn Place, four years after the same venue had witnessed what was reputedly the biggest hit of his career, a muscular drive down the ground that was measured at 140 yards.

But although his ability to draw a crowd would never diminish, by the end of the following decade Grace's powers were in decline. The legend of the man, however, was only just beginning.

'They came to see me bat, not you umpire,' he famously said as he refused to walk after being given out in an exhibition match. He was right. No player did more to develop and popularise the game. English – and Scottish – cricket would not be the same without him.

3

THE INDOMITABLE CARRICK

While WG's appearances in Edinburgh and Glasgow did much to build the profile of cricket in Scotland, James Lillywhite's association with the country would be crowned by a match which featured one of its greatest individual feats. The professional had over 1,200 first-class wickets to his name by the time he appeared for Chichester Priory Park in their game against the touring West of Scotland Cricket Club, but in July 1885 it was the achievement of

Scottish amateur James Stewart Carrick which resonated around the world.

From the time of its foundation in 1862, West of Scotland had established itself as a club of particular repute. Formed by a group of Glasgow businessmen and players from Clutha Cricket Club, which played its matches on the northernmost part of what would become Hamilton Crescent,[*] the West's ambition to be seen as the Scottish equivalent of MCC was soon backed by some impressive performances on the field. Driven by the support of Colonel DCR Carrick-Buchanan[†] and the energy of local tradesman John McNeill – future first President of the Scottish Cricket Union – West of Scotland Twenty-Twos played the All-England Eleven three times in the 1860s, winning by thirteen wickets in 1866 and by twelve three years later.

On 13 September 1878 the profile of the club was elevated still further. One year after the initial Tests in Melbourne – though still four before the international rivalry between England and Australia crystallised itself into the Ashes – the Australians' reciprocal trip to England culminated in their first visit to Scotland as Dave Gregory

---

[*] In addition to hosting a number of international cricket matches as well as prominent domestic games, West of Scotland's home ground was the scene of the world's first football international as, on 30 November 1872, Scotland and England played out a goalless draw. The venue was subsequently used twice more, in 1874 and 1876, when Scotland defeated the Auld Enemy 2-1 and 3-0 respectively.

[†] The West's first President (and dedicatee of DD Bone's *Fifty Years Reminiscences of Scottish Cricket*), Carrick-Buchanan also played a significant role in the establishment of Drumpellier Cricket Club in 1850. He not only offered the club the use of a field on his estate but also arranged for the services of its first professional to be engaged (NL Stevenson: *'Play!'*, p.304). A fast left-arm bowler and noted slip fielder, Carrick-Buchanan played in Scotland's first 'capped' game, a 172-run win over the Gentlemen of Surrey on 10 July 1865. One week later, he opened the batting in Scotland's first ever game at Lord's.

brought his side to Hamilton Crescent for the penultimate leg of what had been a highly successful four-month tour.

With 566 runs at 20.96 Charles Bannerman[*] topped the tourists' batting averages, and after the Australian skipper won the toss and elected to bat against a twelve-strong West of Scotland team, the opener was quickly into his stride again as he put on 48 for the first wicket in the company of his younger brother, Alick. It was Gregory's principal bowler, however, who was destined to steal the show.

Fred Spofforth had played in the second Test in Melbourne,[†] but it was his performance at Lord's at the beginning of the tour which had truly announced his arrival onto the world stage. His match figures of ten for 20 against an MCC team featuring eight current or future England internationals brought him an instant fame which would only be magnified by his glowering presence and evocative moniker. Test cricket's first great fast bowler, 'The Demon' would be quickest to the landmark of fifty international wickets.

The match on 27 May had caused a sensation. Spofforth's haul included both a hat-trick and the wicket of WG Grace, clean-bowled for a second innings duck, as England's most prestigious club was dismissed – in every sense of the word – twice in a single day for scores of 33 and 19.

---

[*] In the inaugural Test in Melbourne, Bannerman scored the first ever Test century, an innings of 165 (retired hurt). In so doing he also accumulated 67.3% of his side's runs, a record which still stands today.
[†] Spofforth had boycotted the first Test in protest at the exclusion of his friend Billy Murdoch from the Australian team.

It was, wrote 'Plum' Warner, a 'severe shock to our complacency … In the space of four-and-a-half hours of actual play, on a very sticky wicket, they defeated a powerful side by nine wickets, and the fame of Australian cricket was established for all time.'[1]

As for Spofforth, he 'jumped about two feet in the air, and sang out: "Bowled! Bowled! Bowled!" [at the wicket of Grace],' recalled his teammate Tom Horan. 'And at the finish in the dressing-room, he said "Ain't I a demon? Ain't I a demon?" gesticulating the while in his well-known demoniac style. Whether or not he christened himself the demon, he certainly was a demon bowler.'[2]

Spofforth began his day in Glasgow by showing the crowd some devilish skills with the bat, however. His innings of 48 was the highest individual score in Australia's total of 268, and although opener Tom Chalmers anchored the reply with a fighting 38, a collapse of five for three left the West on 99 and the match all but over. Following on, the hosts added only 85 more in the face of Spofforth, whose eight for 54 confirmed a win for Australia by an innings and 84 runs. A comprehensive defeat, but, as the tourists' demolition of MCC had shown, hardly a disgrace.

As well as hosting such high-profile occasions, the West also took to the road itself. One such tour was arranged to the south of England in July 1885, taking in five two-day matches against Chichester Priory Park, the Gentlemen of Horsham, the Gentlemen of Sussex, Crofton Wanderers and MCC and Ground. With two games won and three drawn, the results point to a suitably productive trip; a closer look at the first, however, reveals a different kind of accomplishment entirely.

Stewart Carrick* had played for Glasgow against the All-England and United South of England Elevens as a teenager in 1871 and 1872. A return of three ducks and a single from his four innings had not exactly set the heather ablaze, but the following years saw the Blythswood-born left-hander build a reputation as one of the finest batsmen in the country. 'No man in the western district has done more for the game,' wrote DD Bone, 'and made longer scores in the best matches.'[3]

After beginning his career with Glasgow Academicals, Carrick moved on to the Caledonian Club and then, after a break from the game on the demise of the latter in 1876, to West of Scotland. He also shone on the golf course, curling pond and rugby field, on which he won two caps for Scotland at full-back in 1876 and 1877.† A decade later, he was elected President of the Scottish Football Union (the future Scottish Rugby Union) in a further demonstration of the esteem in which he was held. Nothing would surpass his achievement in Chichester, how-

---

*   Carrick sometimes played under the assumed name of JS Robertson, a practice not uncommon in Victorian times as players sought to hide the fact that they were playing cricket rather than working.

†   Lining up alongside Carrick as he made his debut was his West of Scotland team-mate Tom Chalmers. Widely considered to be the first great Scottish full-back, he played in Scotland's first six internationals, all against England, between 1871 and 1876. He was also named on a seventeen-strong shortlist of potential players for the inaugural football international in 1872 after impressing with his goalkeeping skills in a trial match for the Scotland team. In the event, however, every member of the final eleven came from Queen's Park Football Club. Interestingly, Carrick's two appearances for Scotland – against England at the Kennington Oval on 6 March 1876 and in the return match at Raeburn Place on 5 March 1877 – took place on grounds also used for cricket.

ever, as he carried his bat at the city's Priory Park to set a new individual world record score of 419 not out.

'Ten o'clock on Monday morning saw the Scotchmen at practice on the beautiful ground of the Priory Park Club,' recounted the 1886 edition of Percival King's *Scottish Cricketer's Annual*, 'and though the match was to have commenced at eleven o'clock it was nearly noon before Mr J. Carrick [John, elder brother of Stewart] won the toss and sent out his brother and Mr ADR Thomson to oppose the bowling of Lillywhite … and Andrews. The play at first was cautious in the extreme, and runs came slowly. Indeed, throughout the first day's play, the slow scoring was the main feature of the game.

'After about an hour's play the telegraph [scoreboard] showed "sixty up" without the loss of a wicket. Lillywhite had used all his wiles to dissolve the partnership, but without success; changes were adopted, but in vain; still the batsmen continued patient, still the runs came.'[4]

The opening pair settled further as the morning continued. Their early caution had given way to freedom, and by the time lunch arrived Carrick had already brought up his hundred while Thomson stood on the verge of a fifty. The break seemed to disrupt their momentum, however, and as play restarted the pace of the game slowed once more as the batsmen focused on accumulation rather than aggression. Three hundred was passed, but just as it appeared that the pair would end the day unbeaten, Thomson scooped a catch to Henley at cover-point. With the score on 326, he was on his way for 112.

New batsman John Craig* batted out the ten minutes that remained in the day, getting off the mark with a snick for two, while Carrick increased his score with a 'pretty late cut' for three.[5] Stumps were drawn with Carrick unbeaten on 196, Craig on 2, and West of Scotland 331 for one.

After the steady progress of the first day, the second moved things up a gear. Carrick had passed 200 by the time Craig (31) offered a return catch to Heasman, and although John Carrick (15) was also on his way soon after, the West, at 436 for three, had added more than a hundred to its overnight total in rapid time.

The arrival of Archibald Campbell accelerated the scoring still further. Carrick and Campbell, who was given a life after being badly missed at short mid-on, added 164 for the fourth wicket, and when the latter fell for 69 after miscuing Lillywhite to Comber at cover, new man Tom Anderson kept up the pressure on what was, by now, a completely exhausted home attack.

The seventh hundred was passed. Bill Roe's individual world record score of 415† was now in Carrick's sights as he reached his fourth century, but, with the final session nearly over, so too was the end of the match. Umpire Robert Thoms explained what happened next.

'When time had just arrived for drawing stumps,' he wrote to Charles W. Alcock, editor of the weekly publi-

---

* John Craig, a paper manufacturer from Dalkeith, played for the Gentlemen of Edinburgh in their match against the United South of England Eleven at Craigmount Park in 1872. A left-handed batsman and slow right under-arm bowler, he went on to take eleven wickets for Aberdeenshire – including those of both WG Grace and James Lillywhite – as the professionals suffered another defeat on their return north the following year.

† Roe's world record 415 was made in a two-day match between the Long Vacation Clubs of Emmanuel and Caius Colleges at Fenner's, Cambridge, in July 1881.

cation *Cricket*, '[Carrick] had then made 408 runs, but knowing the record was Mr Roe's 415, I asked him privately whether, if Chichester were agreeable, he would then leave off with a not out or keep on and try and beat the record. "Keep on," he replied, which he did until it was beaten.'[6]

Having equalled Roe's score, Carrick passed it with a four to spark memorable scenes.

'Carrick was "shouldered" to the dressing-room amid immense cheering, the spectators exhibiting considerable excitement as soon as it became known that the record was beaten,' recalled the *Annual*. 'The innings was not without chances (there were two – one at the wickets and one at deep mid-on), but considering its duration, the fact that it was against all sorts of bowling throughout two long days – lasting, indeed, from the first ball of the match to the last – it was a wonderful exhibition of patience combined with hard hitting.'[7]

Carrick's one eight – 'a grand square-leg hit' – two sixes, two fives, 30 fours and 34 threes added up to a feat of endurance made all the more impressive by the heatwave conditions prevalent in the south of England at the time.[8] 'What the Priory Park fielders thought about Stuart [sic] Carrick's great innings is not known,' wrote NL Stevenson, 'but can well be imagined.'[9] After two days of chasing leather, coupled with what must have been interminable crossing-over in the field for the left-hander, their fatigue can well be, too.*

---

* The general dominance of ball over bat ensured that the Law allowing an innings to be declared was not introduced until 1889, and was then only permitted from the third day onwards. The first captain to employ the new Law in the English County Championship was Aubrey Smith who, at the County Ground in Hove on 28 May 1890, declared Sussex's second innings closed on 295 for seven against WG Grace's

West of Scotland ended on 745 for four, with Carrick unbeaten on 419 and Anderson on 49. Ten of the Chichester Priory Park eleven had been called on to bowl* as the West 'did much to shake the idea, so firmly held in England, that Scotchmen cannot play cricket.'[10]

In the event, Carrick's record would last for only thirteen months. Andrew Stoddart, a future England captain who, like Carrick, also represented his country at rugby, scored 485 in a single day for Hampstead against Stoics on 4 August 1886, hitting one eight, three fives and 64 fours before being caught at deep point going for his quintuple century as the end of the day approached. Like West of Scotland the year before, Hampstead kept their opponents in the field for the whole of the match; Stoddart, still not done for the day, headed off to play tennis.

On 23 June 1887, Stewart Carrick joined Stoddart as a dual internationalist when he won the first of his eight caps as a Scotland cricketer. His most notable performance for the national team came on familiar territory as, at Hamilton Crescent on 20 June 1889, he scored 112 against Nottinghamshire, thus becoming the only batsman to take a century off the county side in the years between 1887 and 1890. It was an achievement which underlined the quality of one of the most talented sportsmen to have ever worn the Thistle.

'His long and brilliant career as a cricketer has earned the respect of all who love the game,' summarised Bone. 'He, indeed, is a record man, and one of whom Scotland may well feel proud.'[11]

Gloucestershire. All-rounder George Bean then took five for 31, his first-ever five-wicket haul, as Sussex wrapped up a 221-run win.
* From his eighty-five overs, James Lillywhite finished with figures of one for 170.

4

THE GREATEST SCOT

Though JS Carrick will always hold a special place in the history of Scottish cricket, when it comes to the identity of the nation's greatest ever athlete, one man stands alone. The achievements of Leslie Balfour-Melville were truly unique, and no journey through Scottish cricket in the late Victorian and Edwardian eras can be complete without due reference to them. 'Looking to the length of his career, the number of his big scores, and, above all, to the wonderful way in which he has retained, and still retains, his batting powers,' declared *Cricket* in 1913, 'it may fairly be claimed that he more than anyone else holds in Scottish cricket the place held by WG in England.'[1]

Like Grace, Balfour-Melville's cricketing story began in boyhood. Born Leslie Balfour at Bonnington Brae House on 9 March 1854, he was educated at Edinburgh Academy where, after winning a place in the school first XI at the age of fourteen, he rapidly established himself as both its wicketkeeper and leading batsman.

That he did so with some style is clear. In 1870 he was selected to play for the Gentlemen of Scotland against the All-England Eleven, batting for more than an hour against the fast left-arm of James Shaw and Tom Emmett to top score with 17. The innings so impressed George Parr that he asked the youngster to play for the Eleven in their next match in Perth; still being at school, however, he was, 'much against his will,' compelled to decline.[2]

Balfour's earliest cricketing memory went back still further. As a 'small boy in a kilt' in the mid-1860s, he had filled in for the Free Foresters as the wandering team arrived one short for a game against Grange.[3] Batting last against the lobs of Oxford blue RB Ranken he showed both resilience and confidence to remain unbeaten, earning both a promotion up the order for the second innings and an invitation to play for the Foresters again in the process. In 1868 he did so as, even with the schoolboy in its ranks, the team turned up one short again.[4]

After leaving school in 1872, Balfour joined the Foresters' erstwhile opponents. Grange Cricket Club had just taken ownership of its new home at Raeburn Place,* and

---

* After finding itself homeless after twenty-six seasons at Spark's Ground, the venue on Grove Street which had hosted the first visit of the All-England Eleven to

Balfour went straight into the eleven chosen to represent Edinburgh in the two-day game against Glasgow which marked both the official opening of the new ground and the first cricket match between the two cities. Perhaps fittingly the encounter ended in a draw, but not before the eighteen-year-old had put his stamp on the occasion with a second innings score of 150.

'Ever since then he has been the most dangerous batsman on the Grange side,' said *Cricket*. 'In his earlier days … he too often got himself out, being over-fond of hitting at a long hop on the off-side before he got set; but if he did get set, the bowlers were in for a bad time.'[5]

Although not all the scores from his earliest years have been preserved, the records of twenty-nine of the seasons between 1875 and 1910 make for impressive reading. In two hundred completed innings for Grange, Balfour scored a total of 7,653 runs, his highest score of 207 not out coming against Drumpellier in 1893. By now known as Balfour-Melville,[*] his best season of all came ten years later, as 'in spite of wet and difficult wickets' he recorded scores of 145 not out, 108, 103, 100, 76 and 35 in the six innings he played.[6]

He also starred elsewhere. Balfour-Melville played several games for MCC and the wandering team I Zingari, including one at Scarborough against a Gentlemen of England team containing Frederick Spofforth in August

---

Scotland in 1849, Grange played some of its games on Edinburgh Academy's ground at Raeburn Place. Consideration was given to making the arrangement permanent, but this was dismissed in favour of building a new facility on part of Inverleith Farm, located immediately to the east. Work on the site began in 1871, with Grange investing a total of £700 on its new ground and pavilion.

[*] The Balfour family changed its name to Balfour-Melville when Leslie's father succeeded to the estate of Mount Melville, near St Andrews, in 1893.

1888. He was a regular in the 'country house' matches at Glamis Castle, where for many years the Earl of Strathmore's XI played against a variety of invited teams. '"LM" rarely let his side down,' wrote NL Stevenson. 'He hit up several centuries there and at least one double century.'[7]

Noted for the speed at which he accumulated his runs, Balfour-Melville was in many ways a player ahead of his time. His wide repertoire of shots and ability to improvise, as outlined by *Cricket*, featured a level of innovation which pre-echoed the modern game:

'If pitched up, the ball goes to any part of the long field; if a foot short, it is cut or pulled with equal decision. His hitting is often high, but it goes a very long way, and he generally knows where the fielders are. He used often to hit a ball just short of a length on the off over third man's head almost out of the ground, making an upward shot with a vertical bat; but he has given up the stroke as too dangerous. Yorkers were never a terror to him; he was always quick enough to see them and make full pitches of them.

'He also confesses that he does not know what is meant by the "blind spot"; even if a ball beats him, he can see what it is doing. It may be confidently asserted that with [his] powers of physique, arm, and eye he would have been in the highest rank of English batsmen, if circumstances had brought him into first-class cricket.'[8]

Circumstance could easily have taken him in other directions, too. Balfour-Melville would probably have played for Scotland in the inaugural rugby union international in 1871 had he not had the misfortune to be bitten by a dog,[9] but he appeared in the second, against England at the Kennington Oval, on 5 February 1872.* He won the Scottish Lawn Tennis Championship in 1879, the Scottish Billiards Championship and, in 1895, the Amateur Golf Championship, beating the Royal Liverpool Golf Club's John Ball Jr after 37 holes of matchplay on the Old Course at St Andrews. A renowned skater, curler, long jumper and distance athlete, too, Balfour-Melville 'excelled in every game he turned his hand to. [His] perfect hand-eye co-ordination and balance ... meant he strode like a colossus across the scene in the latter half of the nineteenth century.'[10]

Amongst all his accomplishments, though, is one which deserves particular prominence. Balfour-Melville was fully focused on cricketing matters in the summer of 1882, and on 29 July he captained Scotland to a feat which has never yet been repeated: victory over Australia.

Two months into their tour of the British Isles, Billy Murdoch's Australians had arrived in Edinburgh to play a three-day game against Scotland. Billed by *The Scotsman* as the most important match to have yet taken place in the country, the encounter had turned out to be something of a mismatch as the 'invincible cricketers from the antipodes' wrapped up an innings and 18 run victory with more than a day to spare.[11] A one-innings 'fill-up' match was therefore arranged, and so, on an overcast but dry Saturday morning, Scotland and Australia took to Raeburn Place once more.

Despite the nature of the previous loss, 'the prospect of a good day's cricket drew out nearly as large and influential an attendance as on Friday,' reported *The Scotsman*.

---

* Joining the seventeen-year-old Balfour-Melville in the Scotland team were three more cricketers: Tom Chalmers, Henry Renny-Tailyour and Edward Bannerman.

'There were several thousands of people including well-known cricketers from all parts of Scotland with many ladies whose vari-coloured dresses made the scene an animated one.'[12] A selection of rousing tunes from the band of the 3rd Battalion Royal Scots added to the carnival-like atmosphere. Scottish cricket was ready for a story.

After Murdoch won the toss and elected to bat, openers Eugene Palmer and Tom Garrett hit the ground running against Scotland bowlers Peter Thompson and John Craig. The introduction of the fast left-arm of Robert Macnair stopped the advance in its tracks, however, as Palmer was bowled for 18, and with Garrett (28) run out, Sammy Jones (4) bowled and Alick Bannerman (1) caught, Australia's 46 for none had quickly become 55 for four.

Lunch came and went as the collapse continued. Murdoch, coming in at 86 for eight, dragged his team into triple figures, but the fall of last man Charles Beal (7), caught behind by Balfour-Melville off the bowling of David Brown, put the finishing touches onto what had been an impressive Scottish performance. Macnair, with four for 37, and Thompson, with two for 29, took most of the plaudits as Australia was dismissed for 122; having mustered a two innings total of less than 150 in their previous match, however, the Scots knew that when it came to their own batting they could take nothing for granted.

The captain, though, would see them home. Opening the batting with Alfred Wood, Balfour-Melville 'so effectually collared the bowling that 10 and 20 went up rapidly amid cheering', and although Wood (15) offered a return catch to Jones soon after, the arrival of Joseph

Cotterill kept up the momentum.[13] 'Some splendid batting was witnessed,' reported *The Scotsman*, 'both batsmen cutting and driving in fine style'.[14]

Victory was in sight by the time the free-hitting Cotterill (24) skied one to Harry Boyle, and Balfour-Melville duly confirmed it with a mighty blow over square-leg which sailed over the wall and into the adjoining Edinburgh Academy ground. The 'hit of the two matches' brought Scotland its most famous win, and its captain his greatest moment.[15]

With time remaining in the day the hosts batted on, Balfour-Melville continuing to play his shots until he was finally trapped in front by Murdoch for 73. The Australian skipper finished with figures of four for 37, but the day belonged to his opposite number. The Scots closed on 167 for seven as the shadows lengthened, but their eight-wicket win had already been written into cricketing history.

One month later, Australia's victory over England in the one-off Test at The Oval inspired the *Sporting Times* to publish its famous mock obituary of English cricket. 'The body will be cremated and the ashes taken to Australia,' it concluded, little guessing how the concept would catch on.

Leslie Balfour-Melville, meanwhile, continued to serve both club and country until well into the new century. He became the first President of the reformed Scottish Cricket Union in 1909, the same year that he returned, after a sixteen-year hiatus, to captain his country against Ireland in Perth. At the age of fifty-five, he top scored with his international best of 91 as Scotland claimed victory by an innings and 132 runs. In an era often touched by greatness but no less prone to hyperbole as our own, Balfour-Melville was a genuine phenomenon.

Although *Cricket* likened him to WG Grace, a more apt comparison – if one is needed – is with CB Fry. 'He could not exist today,' wrote David Robson of the celebrated English sportsman, politician and writer. 'He possessed an array of talents that have never been equalled.'[16]

In the history of Scottish sport, Leslie Balfour-Melville occupies a similarly exalted place. He could have found fame via any number of avenues. That he, like Fry, chose cricket, is fortuitous indeed.

5

Shadows on the Esk

Just as Hercule Poirot was full of charitable feelings towards the 'old ladies with the maladies', so the sight of Mavisbank House cannot help but bring a rush of similar sentiment today. Decades of neglect have taken their toll on a building once regarded as one of Scotland's finest, but even in its present condition Mavisbank retains the power to impress. A ruin it may be, but no amount of decay can hide the beauty that still remains.

Commissioned by Sir John Clerk of Penicuik – Member of Parliament, lawyer, patron of the arts and one-time pupil of composer Arcangelo Corelli – and designed in collaboration with architect William Adam, Mavisbank was constructed in neoclassical style during the middle years of the 1720s. Located on the banks of the River Esk between the Midlothian communities of Loanhead, Lasswade and Polton, the house was 'both an exemplar of "Roman" living and a beacon of the new post-Union Scotland. It was a cabinet of paintings and sculpture for the intellectual elite of its day, and a haven of private family tranquillity.'[1] Its symmetrical layout, curving wings and elegant ornamentation inspired a new generation of country houses. And through the latter half of the nineteenth century, its grounds gave a home to one of the most renowned cricket clubs in all of Scotland, too.

Just as the passing of time saw Mavisbank fall further into disrepair, so the memory of Lasswade Cricket Club has also grown fainter. There was a time when Lasswade fielded one of best teams in the country, competing with, and beating, some of the biggest names in the game. Today, however, its heyday is remembered only in the passing references of the history books: a once major power now all but forgotten.

In the forty or so years of its existence, Lasswade was one of the most active teams in the country. After beginning its inaugural season modestly with a win over Penicuik and a loss to Glencorse Depot,* the club's fixture

---

* Glencorse Depot was one of the many regimental teams which played against Lasswade over the years. Others included the 3rd Royal Scots, the Royal Scots Greys, the 42nd Highlanders (The Black Watch), the 78th Highlanders, the 31st Hussars, the 7th Hussars, the 1st Royal Dragoons, the 62nd Brigade Depot and the Queen's Edinburgh Rifle Volunteers, several of whom brought their regimental bands with

list expanded rapidly, peaking at around fifty games per season in its later years. 'If Lasswade deserves credit for anything,' remarked 'Mid Off' in the 1888 edition of the *Scottish Cricketer's Annual* (the seventeenth, and final, issue of that landmark publication), 'it is that they have thrown their ground open to all comers, going on the principle "if you can bring eleven men and an umpire, we will play you."'[2]

It was a code which extended to the composition of their team. 'I can very well remember thinking, in the summer of 1869, how very pleasant it would be to form a cricket club at Lasswade; but I was also convinced of the hopelessness of the task,' wrote 'Mid Off'. 'Where were the members to come from? From Lasswade? Well, in eighteen years the village by the peaceful Esk has given us no single member. Contiguity to Edinburgh saved us. Most of the Edinburgh clubs were full of members, cricket grounds were not plentiful, so I suppose there was room for another club.'[3]

It is safe to assume, therefore, that 'Mid Off', unnamed by the *Annual* beyond his nom-de-plume, was one of the three local men – G. Arbuthnot, WA Somerville and JH Annandale – who founded Lasswade in 1869. As he suggests, the club drew many of its cricketers from established Edinburgh teams, while there was also a strong connection with two of the foremost public schools in the area. Many Lasswade players were former pupils of either Loretto – located in Musselburgh – or Edinburgh's Fettes

---

them to Mavisbank to add a musical note to proceedings (J.B. Cairns: *Bright and Early*, 1953, p.123).

College; one, HB 'Tim' Tristram, would go on to become Loretto's third Headmaster in 1903.*

Eight years after the club was founded, Mavisbank House, which had since passed out of the hands of the Clerk family, was reopened as a medical asylum. Staffed by members of the Aesculpian Club, its physicians (who included Dr Joseph Bell, the inspiration behind Sir Arthur Conan Doyle's character of Sherlock Holmes) believed that healing was an art as much as a science, and the house and its grounds accordingly became a private refuge of tranquillity for its well-heeled patients. With its high position affording panoramic views over the surrounding countryside, it was a spot well chosen.

Down by the river in the valley below, the cricket ground was overlooked by Mavisbank's east wing. A number of trees were dotted around the site including a large beech which, in its position at cover-point at the river end of the ground, stopped 'many a lovely cut ... with its stalwart trunk and far-reaching branches.'[4] But despite any difficulties it may have presented in run-scoring, a trip to Mavisbank became a season's highlight for its many visitors.† 'It is a delightful place,' wrote John Thomson in

---

* Both Loretto and Fettes have distinguished cricketing pedigrees both in their own right and through the Fettesian-Lorettonians ('Fet-Lor') Club, the joint team established in 1881. Although recent years have seen a decline in the activities of the 'Fet-Lor', the wider cricketing traditions of both schools continue.

† A host of teams travelled to play at Mavisbank: Grange, Edinburgh University, Edinburgh Academicals, Royal High School, Merchiston Castle, Brunswick, Leith Franklin, Edinburgh Australasians, Watsonians, Carlton, Leith Caledonian, Heriot's, Edinburgh Meadows, Comely Bank, Musselburgh, St Andrews, Kirkcaldy, Dunfermline, Dysart House, Cliftonville, Kingston, Falkirk, Linlithgow, Drumpellier, West of Scotland, Greenock, Alexandria, Selkirk, Abbotsford, Kelso, Galashiels, Berwick, Glenalmond, Blairlodge, Craigmount, Perthshire and Stirlingshire were just some of the teams that joined the local elevens of Bonnyrigg, Dalkeith and Penicuik on Lasswade's calendar. It is a poignant list to study today; around half the teams on it are no more.

his history of Drumpellier Cricket Club. 'We were always handsomely treated when there. Under an old oak tree or stately beech we lunched together. The only fault we had to find with this fixture was that we had to leave so early on account of the train connections.'[5]

That Thomson devoted an entire chapter of his book to Drumpellier's relationship with Lasswade is telling. 'For many years Mr Somerville, along with his nephews – the brothers Caldwell – could give us a good, stiff game,' he wrote. 'We have seen a team pitted against us that could have represented Scotland if necessary.'[6]

Many of Lasswade's players did so. Augustus Asher,* for example, a future County Clerk of Midlothian who also appeared for Grange, played alongside Leslie Balfour-Melville in Scotland's win over the Australians in 1882, while Cambridge blue Andrew 'Bunny' Don Wauchope, another Grange man (and a dual international thanks to his thirteen appearances on the rugby field for Scotland), scored 51 for the national team against WG Grace's Gloucestershire in July 1891.

Don Wauchope had a reputation for consistency. In 1884 he scored six half-centuries including an unbeaten 52 against Edinburgh Academy, while in 1886 he recorded a season's best of 76 for Grange against the Gentlemen of Nottinghamshire as he ended the summer with ten more. 'He is not, in the keenest sense of the term, a brilliant bat,' wrote DD Bone, 'but [he] scores rapidly against good bowling, and rarely fails to make his mark in our leading games.'[7]

---

* In addition to his appearances on the cricket field, 'Gus' Asher was a four-time rugby union international as well as Scottish pole vault champion in 1885 and 1886.

The Loretto-educated Caldwell brothers, Alfred and Herbert, were also capped, Alfred against the Gentlemen of Philadelphia and Herbert against the Parsees. Herbert, a 'capital batsman and fielder' in the words of Bone, had several centuries to his name, and in 1897 scored 519 runs at an average of 32.43 for Lasswade, a tally which included a hundred against Ashburne.[8] A fine driver of the ball, Herbert went on to make several appearances for MCC; both he and his brother, though, were servants of Lasswade first and foremost.

The team's co-founder was also its captain. A paper manufacturer at nearby Kevock Mill, WA Somerville was known throughout Scotland as an under-arm bowler of particular skill. '[He] had a most unusual action,' wrote JB Cairns. 'He took a long run, and, as he ran, his bowling arm moved backwards and forwards with a jerky motion. He then bowled a slow underhand ball which frequently disposed of a too-confident batsman.'[9]

During the 1880s the team also fielded two professionals,[*] the slow and wily Butler and the 'tall, lanky [Frank] Shacklock … who took a long run and delivered balls like greased lightning.'[10] On 14 July 1883, it was Drumpellier which found itself struck down.

The game at Mavisbank had started well for the visitors. Slow right-armer James Buchanan's four for 19, added to Robert Scott's three for 5, saw Lasswade dismissed for just 42, and although Drumpellier lost wickets cheaply in reply, Houston, with 18, steered them to 41 for nine and the brink of victory.

---

[*] Lasswade's first professional, Job Greenwood, was the father of Yorkshire batsman Andrew, who played for England alongside James Lillywhite in the inaugural Test matches in Australia.

'Shacklock was about to bowl when Lasswade's captain,* WA Sommerville [sic],† whispered to him that if he took a wicket without a further run being scored a golden sovereign would be his reward,' recalled Cairns.

'Shacklock's next ball got rid of his man [J. Lindsay] by breaking his middle stump in two, to the great joy of all Lasswade supporters. The two pieces of the wicket were carried in triumph to the pavilion, where they were long kept on view.'[11] It turned out to be Drumpellier's only defeat of the season.

With six wickets for Shacklock and three for Butler it had been another day for the bowlers, while the wicketkeeping of Drumpellier's David Crichton‡ was also praised. 'His stumping of AGG Asher§ from a fast ball of Lindsay's was not seen every day, as also the stumping of Tristram off Buchanan's bowling,' wrote John Thomson, who played in the game. 'Those were two of the best batsmen among the younger generation of cricketers at that time.'

As well as club games, Mavisbank also hosted a number of more social occasions. An annual match was played between Lasswade and the Ladies of Midlothian, pitting the men's team against a women's eleven drawn from local

---

*   In Drumpellier's account of the match, JG Walker is named as the captain that day (John Thomson, *Drumpellier Cricket Club 1850-1906*, 1906, p.115)

†   There is some disagreement between each publication as to the correct spelling of Somerville's name. Four of my sources use 'Somerville', two 'Sommerville'. I have, therefore, sided with the former.

‡   Crichton's one cap for Scotland came at Merchiston Castle in May 1878 in the same match in which Ambrose Dickins, the son of Kelso's Major George, made his sole appearance for the national side.

§   Three years later the twenty-four-year-old Asher scored 170 – an innings which included two hits out of the ground – as Lasswade batted the whole day to score 308 for nine against Clydesdale at Titwood. It was, wrote DD Bone, 'the most remarkable game of 1886 in Glasgow.' (*Fifty Years Reminiscences of Scottish Cricket*, 1898, p.60)

cricketing families. The ladies' team of 3 August 1891, for example, featured five by the name of Cowan together with four Somervilles and two Griersons, all names connected with cricket in either Lasswade or nearby Penicuik.

Certain modifications were made to the playing conditions to ensure an even contest. The gentlemen were handicapped by having to field, bat and bowl left-handed, in addition to using a bat of less than half its usual width. Should the right hand inadvertently be used, six penalty runs were to be added to the ladies' score.

It all made for an exciting game. The ladies, fielding first, dismissed Lasswade for 128, Miss M. Grierson claiming four wickets – all bowled – including that of top scorer EAS Watt for 28. Captain Miss Cowan (the only one of the Cowans not identified by her first name on the scorecard) then led the chase with a free-hitting 38, her fluent scoring supported by 16 from F. Somerville. The latter's departure, however, bowled by Alfred Caldwell, gave Lasswade the upper hand, and although Lily Cowan (12 not out) resisted, Henry Sanderson's seventh wicket confirmed his team's victory as the ladies were finally bowled out for 125.

'With the exception of Mr Sanderson it may be said that the bowling of the gentlemen was not of so high a standard as that of the ladies,' summarised *One Hundred Summers*, the short volume written to commemorate the centenary of Penicuik Cricket Club in 1944. 'There was great excitement at the end when the ladies all but passed the gentlemen's total.'[12]

An additional game was played annually against a twenty-two of local artisans, while a number of touring teams also arranged matches at Mavisbank. The 1887 season, for example, saw Lasswade play, and beat, English sides Trinity College and Salisbury, while in July Gordon Caldwell's 72 not out helped the Scots draw a two-day match against Welsh visitors Bryn-y-Neuadd.* The summer of 1884 brought Lasswade its most notable scalp of all, however, as MCC, fresh from a thumping innings and 115-run win over Australia at Lord's, fell to a 50-run defeat in Midlothian.

That cricket at Mavisbank should end as suddenly as it did, then, is as sad as it is mysterious. The departure of several key members, notably the Caldwells, appears to have been the catalyst, but contemporary accounts furnish little additional detail as to the events which led to the unexpected demise of the club. Precise dates are difficult to ascertain, but by the end of the first decade of the new century, Lasswade Cricket Club was no more.

The *Lorettonian*, the long-established journal of Loretto School, lamented its loss in wistful style.

'The story of Lasswade can only be told by the tongue of a Caldwell. But there are others who have found a joy in playing under the suave command of Somerville, and have watched with interest the wonder and alarm on the batsman's face when the captain began to bowl ... We have heard the lunch bell ring a quarter of an hour early, because seven wickets were down and there was no one else on the field to go in. And then we have adjourned

---

* Lasswade also toured itself, playing such teams as the Lancashire Wizards, Oxford Satellites and English University Wanderers on their visits to England. A reciprocal visit to North Wales to meet Bryn-y-Neuadd was arranged as well as to Ireland, where Lasswade played against North of Ireland, Leinster and Dublin University.

to refresh ourselves beneath the tree, the fairest luncheon pavilion that ever cricket field boasted.

'But all that is past, and it only remains for each one who plays cricket for the sheer love of the game to drop the tribute of a tear over the memory of a club where cricket was played for sport and because men loved it.'[13]

Although those memories grow ever more distant, the traces of Mavisbank's cricketing past are still visible today. Approached along the riverside path, heavily shaded by trees to the right and a high wall to the left, the sudden open expanse of the cricket field is as striking today as it must have been to Lasswade's opponents all those years ago. Many of its trees have been cleared, but the remains of the run-thwarting beech are easily discovered, as are the foundations of the small cricket pavilion which stood in front of the now privately-owned walled garden. A look to the left offers a first glimpse of Mavisbank House itself, now accessible via the restored South Drive.

It is both a beautiful and forlorn sight. Only its façade remains standing, the legacy of a suspicious fire in 1973 which left the building a roofless ruin. Saved from demolition in the 1980s, the long-term interests of Mavisbank House are now overseen by the Mavisbank Trust which, together with Historic Scotland and Midlothian Council, is committed to providing it with a sustainable future. Full restoration is the ultimate goal, and with a suggestion to reinstate the cricket pitch also being explored, one of Scotland's most beautiful grounds may yet be reborn.

And if it is, there will be no more evocative place to play cricket in the country.

6

Highland Games

While Lasswade's star shone all too briefly, that of a second club founded in the same year continues to rise. Breadalbane Cricket Club was one of a flurry to be established in Highland Perthshire during the 1860s, and although many of its companions did not survive the journey into the new century, the Aberfeldy-based team remains a beacon of the game in the region today.

The spread of cricket through the southern Highlands had picked up over the previous decade, but it was the opening of Aberfeldy's railway station in July 1865 which provided the most significant boost to its growth. With five trains a day making the ninety-minute journey to Perth, a new influx of people was brought to the area and it was not long before the Victorian love of clubs and societies began to manifest itself in the formation of cricket teams.

That there was interest in the game was already apparent. The year before, a substantial number of residents had been in Perth when local team Castle Menzies took on Perthshire in a celebratory match arranged to mark the visit of Queen Victoria to the city on 30 August. An innings defeat for the Highland side had followed, but the occasion underlined the growing profile of cricket nonetheless, and the following years saw new teams established in every corner of the region. Dunkeld Cricket Club played its first recorded match in July 1867 against Blairgowrie, while Birnam CC fulfilled its earliest fixtures as a wandering team at around the same time.* Clubs at Pitlochry, Kenmore, Moulin and Amulree were founded, all eager to play each other, and with local travel transformed by the speed and convenience of the railway, the opportunity to do so was as never before.

To their frustration, the citizens of Aberfeldy, however, were being left behind. Despite the town's dual advantage as the largest in the area and the home of its railway station, the absence of a piece of available ground on which to form a club of their own meant that local cricket enthusiasts could only look on in envy as the game grew elsewhere.

A solution, though, was near at hand.

---

* Birnam Cricket Club put down more permanent roots in 1874 on land granted to the club by Mr JB Pople of the Birnam Hotel.

The death of the second Marquis of Breadalbane in 1862 triggered a legal wrangle over who should succeed him. Claim and counter-claim had seen the case rumble on for five years until it was finally decided in favour of the late Marquis' preferred choice, John Alexander Gavin Campbell, who, in due course, became the sixth Earl of Breadalbane.

His son Gavin, a keen cricketer who, as it turned out, would inherit his father's title only four years later, was soon using his newly elevated profile to further the cause of the game. Seeing cricket as an ideal way to bring sport and recreation to Aberfeldy, he arranged for part of the town's East End Park to be gifted for the establishment of a team.

The way was now clear. 'An association has been formed under the most brilliant auspices with the name of the Breadalbane Cricket Club,' announced the *Dundee Courier*, '[which] promises to be highly successful in promoting the physical good of our young men.'[1] Although it turned out to be a while before the new team was able to play regularly in the town, presumably as the ground was prepared to a suitable standard, Breadalbane's 68-run win over Ballinluig CC, played 'in a field a little to the south of the Ballinluig Railway Station' two months after its foundation, featured in the pages of *The Scotsman*.

'The bowling of Messrs S. and J. Keightley [of the] Breadalbane Club was much admired; also the batting of Mr J. Keightley, who scored 44 [out of Breadalbane's total of 88],' the newspaper reported. In bowling their opponents out for just 20, 'the fielding of the Breadalbane Club was much superior to that of the Ballinluig', too.[2] The new club was off to a good start.

Almost a year later, appearing alongside the story of a large whale which had been spotted in the bay at St Andrews, Breadalbane's trip to play Ivanhoe CC also made the papers. While parties of Fifers gleefully took to their boats to take pot-shots at the poor creature, Breadalbane's day at Stobb's Muir was ending in a 55-run defeat as they were dismissed for a two-innings total of just 58 on 2 July 1870.

The same decade saw John C. Campbell play his first match for the club. A future captain of the side, his unpublished memoir adds further colour to the story of Breadalbane's early days.

'An amusing incident happened when [Breadalbane] was playing Pitlochry ... [in] about the year 1886,' he recalled. 'The BCC bowler at one end had taken two wickets with two successive balls, and the next man in was a Sandhurst cadet who swaggered in, smoking his pipe. The day was rather chilly and he had on his blazer and sweater. When he arrived at the crease he proceeded to doff first his blazer then his sweater, both of which he gave to the umpire. He then rolled up his sleeves, took centre, had a long lingering look all round the field, did a little gardening, removed little obstacles from the wicket and finally took the pipe out of his mouth and laid it behind the stumps.

'Meantime, Breadalbane's captain, Professor Harrower, who watched this amusing interlude, came over to the bowler and offered him a brand new hat if he bowled the cadet next ball and complete the hat-trick. The bowler obliged by sending the middle stump flying. The batsman then proceeded to pick up his pipe and collect his chattels.'[3]

As Breadalbane established itself, the wider game continued to expand. Teams at Taymouth and Methven were formed, joining the Dundee Travellers (a group of holidaymakers from the city who met up to play cricket each summer) and the Gentlemen of Strathtay (a team which included members of the famous Playfair family) in an ever-widening exchange of fixtures.[*]

Matches were also arranged against teams associated with the large country properties. The Garth estate, for example, had been purchased in 1880 by the Greenock-born politician and shipping magnate Sir Donald Currie. A great enthusiast for the game, Sir Donald employed a large number of students from Oxford University to work on his land each summer and, having carefully checked their cricketing credentials beforehand, he fielded a team which played regularly against Breadalbane during the last two decades of the century.[†]

Most anticipated of all, though, was the club's annual visit to Dall House, residence of Captain Bruce Canning Vernon-Wentworth, on the south side of Loch Rannoch. Conveyed there by four-in-hand carriage and the steam launch SS *Gitana*, the team enjoyed a lavish day out with extensive hospitality as well as a beautiful pitch upon which to play.

---

[*] Another team active on the circuit was that of the Murthly Lunatic Asylum – 'made up of staff, rather than patients,' clarified Mark Bridgeman – which continued to play against Breadalbane until the 1950s. The hospital, opened in 1864, had a beautifully kept cricket pitch within its grounds to encourage exercise amongst its residents.

[†] Sir Donald also has a lasting connection with rugby union as the founder of the Currie Cup, South Africa's most prestigious rugby competition.

Their host was no mean cricketer himself. In addition to scoring 180 for the Household Cavalry – an innings, it is said, he never tired of recalling – Captain Vernon-Wentworth made three first-class appearances for MCC, and in the gala matches at Dall House there was no doubt at all as to who the star turn was intended to be.

'It must have cost a fair amount, this all-expenses-paid, ridiculously posh trip every year, but Vernon-Wentworth was clearly very keen on putting on a show for the benefit of his watching guests,' said Breadalbane historian Mark Bridgeman, 'and because he was a really good, experienced cricketer, he would duly thrash a century against these yokels from Breadalbane and everyone would go away suitably impressed.'

The Dall House matches feature prominently in John Campbell's memoir, which also hints at the rivalry underpinning what was, on the surface at least, a predominantly social occasion.

'[In around] 1884, an incident took place in one of the matches at Dall House in which a dispute arose as to what constituted a no-ball and which interrupted the progress of the game,' he wrote. 'A Breadalbane bowler, when delivering the ball over the wicket, knocked down the bails with his heel and the batsman, Lord Apsley, was caught at mid-off. The Dall players claimed a no-ball and Breadalbane held that it was not and that the player was out. The game was suspended and Dall House searched for a copy of *Lillywhite's Annual*, containing the rules [sic]. [Once] this was found and carefully scrutinised … and our opponents were convinced that the umpire's decision was a correct one,* the game was then amicably resumed.'⁴

The loss of SS *Gitana* to a storm shortly after Campbell completed his account brought a sad end to Breadalbane's Dall House excursion. Much worse was to follow, though, as the onset of the new century saw a different kind of ill-wind blow through the southern Highlands.

'So much of the history of cricket in Highland Perthshire is tied to the economic story of the area,' said Mark Bridgeman, 'and the decision of the Government to impose a 40% estate duty on any property worth over £2,000,000 had a drastic effect. The estate at Castle Menzies went bankrupt, Garth and Atholl too. These were all places which fielded cricket teams which also then fell by the wayside.

'Ballinluig and a few of the other smaller clubs had already folded or been forced to merge by the turn of the century, and with a number of Aberfeldy's players now having to move away from the area to find work, Breadalbane suddenly found itself in difficulties, too.'

In 1905, sharing a page with news of am-dram rehearsals and a progress report on the repainting of Alyth Parish Church – both featured in a section entitled 'Over the Teacups: Notes of Interest to Our Women Readers' – the *Dundee Evening Post* previewed the forthcoming cricket season. After assessing the respective prospects of England and Australia in the upcoming Ashes as well as the domestic chances of Forfarshire, Perthshire and the rest, attention was turned to the situation in Aberfeldy.

---

* It was not until 2013 and the misfortunes of England's Steven Finn that MCC finally decided that a change in the Law regarding the stumps being disturbed by the delivery stride of the bowler was needed.

'Why there is not a first class [sic] cricket club in Aberfeldy is very hard to tell,' the column reads. 'Breadalbane Cricket Club, which at one time had many excellent players who did not fail to give a good account of themselves, has been defunct for about three years. Last year a number of enthusiasts started the Aberfeldy Cricket Club, with Mr Charlie Robertson as captain and Mr Charles S. Bain as secretary. This club played two matches during last season, and at those matches it was perfectly evident that there were quite a number of really good cricketers in the town, if only a little more enthusiasm could be worked up.'[5]

'The newspaper's belief that next to no cricket had been played in Aberfeldy for three years wasn't strictly true,' said Mark Bridgeman. 'Granted, the club wasn't fulfilling a regular fixture list, but teams had been put out for friendlies and such like. The report is also a little misleading in that Aberfeldy Cricket Club and Breadalbane Cricket Club are essentially two names for the same thing.

'But matters were clearly beginning to move in the right direction again. Fundraising events for the club were organised in 1905 and 1906, and in due course the reformed Breadalbane joined the North Perthshire League.'

With a side that included James Soutar, reputedly the fastest bowler in Scotland, as well as four more who played for the national team – Joseph Anderson, George Chalmers, Angus McGregor and Charles Mannes, a formidable batsman who played against West Indies in 1906 and the South Africans in 1907* – the rejuvenated club hit the

---

* Mannes also played club cricket for Drumpellier – he received a standing ovation at Mavisbank after scoring 114 out of Drumpellier's total of 187 against Lasswade on 13 June 1891 – and was part of the West of Scotland team which posted 745 for four

ground running, claiming the league title in 1907 and the runner-up spot a year later. The summer of 1909 saw a new individual scoring record established by WL Wood, whose innings of 137 against Glenalmond set a benchmark which would last into the modern era. Breadalbane Cricket Club was back in business.

The 1909 season also brought an extra injection of publicity thanks to the touring Australians. On their way back from a visit to Taymouth Castle – seat of the Marquis of Breadalbane – Monty Noble's Ashes squad made an unscheduled stop-off in Aberfeldy.

The *Dundee Evening Telegraph* related the story in exquisitely parochial fashion.

'A party of Dundonians staying at the Breadalbane Hotel had yesterday a pleasant finish put to their weekend by the arrival of the Australian cricketers. The distinguished sportsmen had on Sunday taken tea with the Duke of Fife and the Princess Royal at Mar Lodge, and they came on from Braemar in a little procession of beflagged motors, through landscapes glorious with sunlight and autumn colours.

'After lunch, the sportsmen made merry in the square treating the interested spectators to a display of trick fielding. The Dundonians were assured by the Australians that they were thoroughly enjoying their pleasure tour through Scotland and Noble and [Warwick] Armstrong courteously permitted themselves to be snapshotted.'[6]

That such a large number of day-trippers had made the journey from Dundee may well have been down to more than a desire to take in the local scenery. The October

---

at Chichester Priory Park in July 1885. On that occasion, perhaps fortunately for the beleaguered Sussex team, he was not required to bat.

holiday meant that all the city's pubs were closed. 'Quietness reigned throughout the city,' reported the *Telegraph*, 'and the police had an easy time.'[7]

But no-one could have predicted the abruptness with which peace would be shattered only five years later. The onset of the Great War changed every aspect of life in Scotland, and although a much-weakened Breadalbane managed to reform in the aftermath of the Armistice to play friendly cricket against other local teams, the happy innocence of its early years had been lost for good. From the Borders to the Highlands and beyond, the golden age of Scottish cricket was over. Nothing would ever be quite the same again.

7

On the Promise of the Fruit

To many, Archie Jackson was the greatest batsman of them all. His delicate leg-side play, wristy flicks and balletic footwork drew comparisons with the great Victor Trumper and, for an all too brief time, provided an elegant counterpoint to the level-headed resolve of his Australian teammate Donald Bradman. Jackson's tragically early death robbed the cricketing world of a player to whom similar immortality beckoned. 'Some batsmen accumulate and others grind,' wrote Alex Massie, 'but the elegance and grace with which Jackson danced at the crease left even his victims with little choice but to admire the style with which he put them to the sword.'[1]

Jackson was blessed with every gift bar the one most precious of all: that of time. We will never know for sure what he would have achieved had tuberculosis not intervened, but in one matter, at least, there is certainty. No finer cricketer was ever born in Scotland.

The Jackson family home was at 1 Anderson Place in Rutherglen when young Archibald[*] made his entrance on 5 September 1909. His parents Sandy and Margaret already had two daughters; a third, Jeanie, would join Lil, Peggie and Archie after the First World War.

Sandy Jackson also had a connection to Australia. He had lived there with his parents as a teenager, and now, with a growing family to support, he decided to make a return. In February 1912 Sandy swapped Rutherglen for Sydney, paving the way for the rest of his family to follow on the steamer *Themistocles* eighteen months later. Archie celebrated his fourth birthday in the Sydney suburb of Balmain; when he next saw the land of his birth, it was as an Australian Test cricketer.

Archie was not the first in his family to make his mark as a sportsman. His uncle Jimmy played football for Glasgow Rangers, Newcastle, Woolwich Arsenal and West Ham, while two of his cousins were also professional players. The elder, James, made over 200 appearances for Liverpool, while Archibald (a second Archie) played at centre-half for Sunderland, Tranmere Rovers and Accrington Stanley. Out in Australia, young Archie would

---

[*] Archie was not christened with a middle name, but in later years he adopted that of his father, Alexander. Scorecards thereafter refer to him as AA Jackson.

shine on the football field, too, being good enough to play for New South Wales Schoolboys, but it was with Balmain District Cricket Club that he truly excelled. Archie made his first appearance for the club as a fourteen-year-old in the 1923-24 season; by the start of the next, he was a fixture in the first team.

Two summers later, at the age of seventeen, Archie made his debut for New South Wales. His first season of Sheffield Shield cricket brought him 464 runs at an average of 48, while his second saw him score two centuries in a single match, a feat no batsman of his age had achieved before. On 1 February 1929 he opened the batting in his Test debut for Australia against England in Adelaide, standing firm in the face of Harold Larwood and Maurice Tate as Australia slipped to 19 for three before leading the counter-attack with a style and confidence which belied both his age and the situation. Resuming on 97 after the lunch interval, he was advised by his batting partner, Donald Bradman, to take his time and play himself back in. Jackson responded by crashing Larwood's next delivery to the cover-point boundary to bring up his hundred.

'That glorious stroke has lived in my memory to this day for its ease and perfect timing,' remembered Larwood. 'I am sure that few among the many thousands present sighted the ball as it raced to the boundary.'[2] Jackson went on to score 164.* Australia lost the Test, and ultimately the series, but gained a new star.

An innings of 182 in the Test trial at the Sydney Cricket Ground made certain of his place on the 1930 tour

---

* At nineteen years and 149 days, Jackson became the youngest Test centurion. He held the record until Giff Vivian reached three figures for New Zealand against South Africa on 4 March 1932 at the age of nineteen years and 121 days.

to England, and despite the presence of Bradman – who scored 124 and 225 in the same match – it was Jackson who drew the crowds as the team landed at Dover. The *Sydney Mail* epitomised Australian confidence: 'On Australian wickets, and judged solely on stroke technique, Archie Jackson may be justifiably regarded as the greatest of present-day batsmen – greater even than Walter Hammond … He was not forced, as was Hammond repeatedly, to look for runs in one direction.'[3] Considering that Hammond had scored 905 runs at an average of 113.12 in Australia the previous summer, it was quite a statement.

As the team acclimatised to English conditions in the nets at Lord's, Jackson went through his repertoire of cuts and drives for an admiring audience of onlookers. 'He looks like any English public school boy, is quiet, and a little shy,' observed the correspondent from the *Evening News*. 'There is something of the Hobbs about Jackson, the stylist.'[4]

But while Bradman began his tour with 236 against Worcestershire, Jackson struggled to find form – and, more ominously, good health – in the unsettled late spring weather. Always susceptible to viruses, the damp air brought on frequent bouts of illness, and though glimpses of his ability were always there, consistency, let alone a big score, eluded him. After sitting out the first two Tests, an innings of 79 against Larwood and Voce at Trent Bridge put Archie into the team for Headingley, but, opening with Bill Woodfull, he managed only a single before offering a dolly to Larwood at short-leg. Bradman, next in, scored a new Test record 334: a combination of rain, bad light and Wally Hammond salvaged a draw for England.

While the result left the series nicely poised at one-all, it had been a less than happy experience for Archie thus far. There was some compensation off the field as his cousin James got in touch, enabling the two to spend a pleasant day in Liverpool together, but it must have been particularly special when, immediately after the conclusion of the match in Leeds, the tour party travelled on to Edinburgh.[5] By late evening on 15 July, more than seventeen years after he had boarded the *Themistocles*, Archie Jackson was back on Scottish soil once more.

The following day he was also back on the field for the Australians' game against Scotland at Raeburn Place. Unfortunately, however, only two hours play was possible before heavy rain sent the players running to the pavilion.

The game had already promised much. After choosing to bat first in conditions which offered plenty to the visiting bowlers, Scotland's batsmen had started well in reaching 129 for three. Clarrie Grimmett and Percy Hornibrook were a particular handful on the already damp pitch but, as *The Scotsman* observed, the home top-order had shown little fear in taking the attack to Australia's front-line spinners. 'Both [bowlers] had to be carefully watched, but it was shown that both could be hit, even Grimmett, who has been so successful in England … Though he nearly bowled both of Scotland's opening batsmen round their legs, and beat them without hitting the wicket, his two victims [John Kerr (20) and Alastair McTavish (35)] were claimed at considerable expense.'[6] Aberdeenshire's Gilbert Alexander, captain of the home team, made a half-century.

The following day was completely washed out, and, to the frustration of the crowds which continued to appear, the match was finally abandoned after lunch on the third day. 'A considerable number of people were waiting at the gates, which were never opened,' *The Scotsman* reported. 'There was keen disappointment in cricket circles in Edinburgh over the fact that no opportunity had been afforded of seeing the Australians batting, and particularly so as in the late afternoon the weather was fine.'[7] Even then, Scottish cricket's particular version of Murphy's Law had a finely tuned sense of mischief.

It is easy to imagine the exasperation which Archie must also have felt at being deprived of a chance to play himself into form in his homeland, and as the Australians moved on to Hamilton Crescent on 19 July the sight of yet more rain would have done little to lift his spirits. After a delayed start the teams dodged more showers throughout the day, the Scotland XI eventually reaching 140 for six in the three-and-a-half hour's play which was possible. 'There was an attendance of about 7,000,' reported *The Scotsman*, 'and as between 5,000 and 6,000 of them would pay two shillings admission money, the Scottish Cricket Union would do pretty well financially despite the broken weather. The afternoon rain, however, would keep many away.'[8]

But to the relief of all the rest day on 20 July saw the weather begin to turn, and after Scotland declared on its overnight total the Australians at last had a chance to bat. A crowd of 8,000 paid their two shillings to watch the tourists rack up an entertaining 337 for nine.

Bradman continued his remarkable run with yet another century. 'His stay was one of nearly two hours and a half,' *The Scotsman* observed, 'and in putting together his 140 he was seen in three distinct moods. There was a sample of the real Bradman when, without any flurry or fuss, and to all appearance no great effort, he scored at a rapid rate; he was seen, too, as if he could not force the ball away; and then again he joined in a lively spell of hitting at almost every ball which was pitched up at all well.'[9] After nineteen boundaries and one six (a comparative rarity in the Bradman canon – The Don was a player who liked to hit the ball along the ground), 'he practically threw away his wicket.'[10] Grange's Sandy Baxter, on his way to figures of four for 89, was the grateful recipient.

After Alan Kippax (0) was also dismissed, Archie Jackson had his opportunity. Less than seven miles from his childhood home, he began what would be his only innings in Scotland.

Batting alongside Ted a'Beckett, the score advanced to 291 before the all-rounder was stumped off Ben Tod for 43. It had been a fruitful if cautious partnership, with both batsmen taking 'some good-humoured barracking from the crowd', but Jackson had shown enough to warrant an appreciative write-up.[11] 'After Bradman,' opined *The Scotsman*, 'Jackson was probably the soundest and most attractive cricketer of the whole eleven.'[12] After batting for over two hours, he remained unbeaten on 52 as the match was drawn.

'The wicket probably was too wet and lifeless for the batsmen, and it could not have given any great aid to the bowlers,' the report summarised. 'There was little or no sun, and the pitch, which was newly prepared yesterday morning, seemed to go easy all day. The Saturday wicket had been too seriously affected by the weekend rain to be played upon.'[13]

For Archie, though, his return to Scotland had been a special experience, and the following day he described it in a letter to his Balmain teammate Bill Hunt.

'We have just concluded our trip to Scotland and everyone had a marvellous time,' he wrote. 'Of course I had some relatives there and had to look them up. They were living at Gourock, a small village twenty miles from Glasgow on the River Clyde, and we had a wonderful view of many famous Lochs and beauty spots such as Dunoon, where Harry Lauder resides, Rothesay, Loch Long and Loch Lomond.'[14] He signed off with a promise to himself to return north after the tour was over.

Although his innings in Glasgow had not been enough to see him keep his place for the fourth Test at Old Trafford (where rain and bad light ensured another draw), Archie was recalled to the side for the fifth Test at The Oval after scoring 118 in the Australians' tour match at Taunton. There he played his most important Test innings of all as, on a treacherous pitch and with Larwood at his spiciest, he added 243 for the fourth wicket with Bradman. Jackson's share was a courageous 73 as Australia won its first Test at The Oval since Spofforth's 'Ashes match' of 1882 and, with it, the famous urn once more.

It was becoming increasingly apparent, however, that Archie was far from well. Back at home, he struggled through the early stages of the series against West Indies before being dropped after the fourth Test in Melbourne. The game at the MCG proved to be his last first-class appearance.

A diagnosis of pneumonary tuberculosis was made. Archie fought on, playing when he could and writing a column for Brisbane's *Daily Mail* when he couldn't, but by February 1933 it was clear that he was dying. Confined to Ingarfield Private Hospital in Brisbane, a short distance from the Gabba where the fourth Test of what would become known as the Bodyline series was getting underway, he summoned the strength to send his old adversary Harold Larwood a telegram of congratulations. It proved to be one of his final acts. As 16 February dawned, the very day that England regained the Ashes it had lost in 1930, Archie Jackson passed away. He was twenty-three.

His body returned to Sydney on the same train which carried the Australian and English teams back to New South Wales for the final Test of the series. Thousands lined the streets to pay their respects as the pall-bearers – Bill Woodfull, Vic Richardson, Donald Bradman, Bert Oldfield, Stan McCabe and Bill Ponsford – carried Archie's casket to its final resting place in the Field of Mars Cemetery. 'He played the game,' reads his headstone. That he did, but, for the greatest of all of Scotland's cricketing sons, all too fleetingly.

8

English Captain, Scottish Heart

While affection for Archie Jackson transcended national boundaries – his death-bed telegram to Harold Larwood remained the bowler's most treasured possession – the bitterness of the on-field rivalry between England and Australia has come to be personified by the man who was Larwood's captain. The name of Douglas Jardine still polarises opinion today, and with the Ashes more keenly contested than ever, it seems destined to justify future accusations of underhand Poms or whinging Aussies for as long as the series continues to be played.

England's tactics during the Bodyline tour of 1932-33 steered cricket into previously uncharted waters, but when it comes to the part played by the skipper at the helm there is, at least, one point upon which both sides agree. Jardine, they say, was the embodiment of his nation: England expected, and, for better or worse, its captain did his duty.

A fly is swimming in the ointment of that neatly packaged summary, however. English icon he may be, but the heart of Douglas Jardine lay very much to the north of Hadrian's Wall.

That he was born in Bombay (now Mumbai) on 23 October 1900 matters little. In the days of Empire it was not unusual for British nationals to spend the entirety of their working lives in India or the colonies, often sending their children home to be educated while maintaining their own bond with the mother country through the turnings of their social circle. To that extent, it cannot be said that Douglas' birthplace made him any less of a Scot; on the contrary, in fact, his sense of Scottishness was only deepened by his Indian upbringing.

His father Malcolm, himself Indian-born, had returned to the country to practise law in 1893 after completing his education at Balliol College, Oxford. British lawyers dominated the legal system of the time and Malcolm's rise through the ranks would culminate in his appointment to the position of Advocate General of Bombay in 1915.

The accomplished lawyer was also an excellent cricketer. Educated at Fettes College, Douglas' father topped the averages in both batting and bowling as captain of the first XI in 1888, and after leaving school he became a leading light in the 'Fet-Lor' Club, the joint team established with former pupils of Loretto.

Malcolm became a first-class cricketer in 1889 when he was selected to play for the University against the Gentlemen of England. He would appear in forty-six first-class matches in all, mainly for Oxford and Middlesex, and score a total of 1,439 runs, but his call to the Bar the following year ensured that his future cricketing career would be an intermittent one.*

In the manner of his upbringing, Douglas followed his father down what was a well-trodden path for a child of the Empire. Leaving India and his parents behind, the nine-year-old Douglas was sent to St Andrews to stay with his Aunt Kitty prior to beginning his education at Horris Hill prep school in 1910. Sunnymede, her house on St Leonard's Road, would become home for the majority of his school holidays, and although life must have been tough for a young boy so far from familiarity, he later wrote of his abiding affection for 'that old grey city by the sea.'[1]

A significant part of Douglas' bond to the historic Fife town was forged through his friendship with a man who became both a mentor and surrogate father during those

---

* Malcolm Jardine also appeared for Scotland against Ireland in 1890, but, despite being given the opportunity to do so, his son did not follow in his footsteps. Minutes from the Scottish Cricket Union Committee show that Douglas was twice selected to play for Scotland (against Australia at Raeburn Place in 1930 and for two matches against South Africa in 1935) but declined to do so on both occasions. His reason why is not recorded, although the small number of matches he played in the years that followed his final appearance for England provides an illustration of the disillusionment he undoubtedly felt towards the game in the aftermath of the Bodyline controversy.

impressionable early years. Well into his seventh decade by the time Douglas arrived in Scotland, the poet and folklorist Andrew Lang took the young boy under his wing, spending hours with him in deep discussion of the finer points of the 'two "Cs" – Cricket and Classics,' as Jardine later recalled, 'the two most important things in the world.'[2]

'St Andrews ... which is the home and cradle of golf, always reckoned Mr Lang "a bit of a character",' he continued. 'Perhaps it was his incurable loyalty to cricket – in spite of his environment – that earned him this reputation in a town which was not lacking in "characters". Indeed, I think that Mr Lang was living up to his reputation when he extended his friendship to a very small boy and heaped kindnesses upon his head.'[3]

Although Oxford University, Surrey County Cricket Club and, in due course, England would take him elsewhere, Jardine's bond to Scotland remained. His daughter Fianach – named after the small Sutherland lochan from which her father caught his first trout – recalled how 'ferociously proud' he was of his ancestry, a family sentiment maintained wholeheartedly by his children.

Fianach inherited many of her father's other qualities, too. Generous and principled, the eldest of his four children worked as a graphic designer in London before moving to Clackmannanshire, where, in time, she trained for the priesthood. She ministered at the St James the Great Episcopal Church in Dollar for several years before her death in 2013.

Her partner John McCabe still lives in the nearby village of Muckhart today. Softly spoken, thoughtful and with a ready chuckle, he told me of Fianach, Scotland and her memories of her father.

'Fianach always felt that he was kind and loving but somewhat remote,' he began. 'Mr Jardine didn't always see his children because of work, or the War when that came, and of course he had been sent to boarding school when he was a child so he was brought up to be not that close to his family. He was extremely self-contained – a late Victorian in terms of his attitudes, I suppose.

'But all his daughters were crazy about him. They knew that any sense of remoteness wasn't his fault and they certainly didn't hold it against him.'

Although Douglas and his wife Isla settled their family in the south of England, they were frequent visitors to Scotland, often holidaying at Crosscraigs, the 25,000-acre estate in Highland Perthshire rented each summer by Sir Harry Peat, the children's maternal grandfather.*

'Scotland always felt like home to Fianach,' said John. 'She adored her grandfather, and the family spent many summer holidays at the estate where the children learned to fish and stalk and so on. They were very happy times.'

Their father must have been equally delighted, especially since it gave him the opportunity to introduce his children to his favourite pastime of all. Jardine devoted an entire chapter of his account of the Bodyline tour to fishing, a pursuit he had discovered under the tutelage of Andrew Lang and which proved to be particularly therapeutic during the tumultuous events that unfolded Down

---

* Sir Harry was a partner in his father's company William Barclay Peat & Co which, after becoming Peat, Marwick, Mitchell and Co in 1925, merged with Klynveld Main Goerdeler in 1987 to form the accounting firm KPMG, one of the so-called 'Big Four' auditors of today.

Under. 'There is no better way of seeing a country, or of forgetting the troubles of life,' he wrote.[4]

The 'troubles' to which Jardine was subjected remained a cloud from which he never truly escaped. Devised to counter the threat of Donald Bradman, Bodyline tactics involved the bowling of fast, short-pitched deliveries on or outside the line of leg-stump – the 'line of the body' – with a close ring of catchers placed behind square on the leg-side to take advantage of any mistake from the batsman as he took evasive action. The England captain despised the term 'Bodyline' (an expression coined by the newspapers), insisting instead on the technical – and less emotive – description of 'leg-theory'.

Seen in Australia as overly aggressive, the accusation that England's tactics were 'unsportsmanlike', made in a cable from the Australian Board of Control to MCC during the third Test in Adelaide, infuriated the governing body in London and very nearly led to the cancellation of the remainder of the tour. The allegation was hastily withdrawn but the febrile atmosphere, whipped up by an exceptionally hostile press, even spilled into the diplomatic arena, putting wider Anglo-Australian relations under strain. 'No politics ever introduced in the British Empire ever caused me so much trouble as this damn Bodyline bowling,' grumbled JH Thomas, Secretary of State for the Dominions.[5]

MCC, having initially responded bullishly to the cabled protests of the Australian Board of Control (ABC), began to shift its position on the tourists' return. Although it is inconceivable that the powers-that-be knew nothing of their captain's plans in advance, the governing body's need to distance itself from the controversy meant that the on-field protagonists of Bodyline would have to pay the price. Harold Larwood, who ended the tour with thirty-three wickets, never played for his country again after refusing to sign a written apology for his bowling in Australia. Jardine, meanwhile, who had since scored a century for England against a West Indian Bodyline-style attack led by Learie Constantine and Manny Martindale, declared himself unavailable for the home Ashes series as the summer of 1934 approached. In saving MCC the trouble of removing him themselves, he had bowed to the inevitable. The ostracism of England's captain and number one fast bowler had begun.

Speaking back in 2006, Fianach gave a hint as to the private toll it exacted upon her father.

'He had a lovely dry sense of humour and used to love reading Kipling's *The Jungle Book* to my brother, two sisters and myself before we went to sleep at night. But he had a sadness about him right up until his death in 1958,' she told *The Daily Telegraph*.

'He was never angry about the furore surrounding Bodyline but, yes, there was this distinct air of sadness more than anything else in that Father believed he had done what the MCC had agreed to. He felt that having said one thing, when the going got really difficult the MCC made him the fall guy. Father was shy, reserved, a terribly gentle man with a strict sense of fair play who wouldn't dream of stretching the rules during a family game of Ludo, never mind on the cricket pitch.'[6]

'Fianach was indignant about the whole Bodyline saga, especially with regard to MCC and the way in which they tried to blame Mr Jardine for their own rather stupid plans,' said John McCabe. 'When the team tried the so-called Bodyline style of bowling in the first Test, one of the Australian batsmen [Stan McCabe] scored a hundred off it, so it was a bit late when the Aussies started whinging about it afterwards.

'Fianach never blamed MCC for her father's death – that wasn't fair – but she certainly felt that what happened didn't help him come to a long, happy and healthy retired life. Mr Jardine took it all on the chin and didn't say anything because he was a gentleman, but he was made a scapegoat.

'They won that series by four to one, for goodness sake. Anyone else would have received a knighthood, but he was pilloried.'

That Jardine retained the loyalty and affection of his team and the firm friendship of many Australians, too, flies in the face of the received wisdom surrounding Bodyline.

'Bob Menzies, who became Australia's longest-serving Prime Minister, got on very well with Mr Jardine,' said John. 'They were the best of friends and would get together whenever he visited this country. Mr Jardine's friendship with [Australian Test cricketer and Bodyline veteran] Jack Fingleton doesn't sit well with all the Bodyline mythology, either. So there was a conflict between the Australian press who didn't like Mr Jardine or his tactics and a lot of Aussies who didn't seem to mind very much.'

Archie Jackson, through his column in the Brisbane *Daily Mail*, was another who belonged with the latter.

'Other writers have said that Ponsford and Fingleton have been battered unmercifully about the body,' he wrote during the series. 'That is mostly their own fault. Fingleton, like Woodford, is a flat-footed batsman … Bradman and McCabe, on the other hand, have hardly felt the impact of leather on flesh, primarily because their movements are snappy enough to allow them to glide to the off-side and allow the balls to fly harmlessly by.

'For the sake of Australia's sporting traditions, may it be left to the cricketers themselves to furnish the only answer to the legitimate tactics employed by the Englishmen.'[7]

Regardless of such sentiments, public hostility to Bodyline reached such a level that Jardine was moved to appeal to the ABC to act against the 'offensive' and 'thoughtless' barracking coming from the stands. He himself was the target of much of it, but Fianach offered an alternative take on the popular impression of a humourless, out-of-touch captain holding himself aloof from the paying public.

'I remember there being something on the television a few years ago about so-called sledging in cricket, and Fianach just burst out laughing, saying, you've no idea what they called my father!' said John. 'But she did point out that during the tour he would deliberately wear his Harlequins cap. Her father was getting all this abuse from the crowds so he wore this hat just to wind them up that little bit more.'

The Oxford blue, maroon and buff cap of Oxford University's Harlequins Cricket Club became a symbol of what the Australian crowds viewed as the England captain's stiff, ultra-establishment persona. That the England team's impromptu dress code was reversed in the final tour game, however, with Jardine wearing the official MCC cap while his teammates took to the field in a colourful collection of 'jazz hats', adds weight to Fianach's description of the twinkle in the eye behind her father's motives.

After serving with the Royal Berkshire Regiment during the Second World War, where he was amongst the last in his regiment to be evacuated from Dunkirk – 'Mr Jardine's main comment [on the evacuation] was that most of the damage done to the British troops was not by the German Messerschmitts but by the bloody British pilots who couldn't see right' – Jardine found work in the City, and by the mid-1950s was contemplating retirement to a plot of land he had bought on the outskirts of Salisbury, the capital of what was then Southern Rhodesia.

In late 1957, however, his close-knit family was turned upside down. After struggling to shake off a bout of tick fever he had contracted in Africa, further tests revealed him to be in the advanced stages of lung cancer. Douglas and Isla travelled to a clinic in Switzerland in the hope of treatment, only to find that the disease had spread and was incurable. The end, when it came, was swift. Douglas Jardine died in Montreux on 18 June 1958.

'Fianach always regretted the fact that she wasn't with her father when he died,' said John. 'They were very close and she cherished her memories of him, particularly of the first time he took her to Lord's. Fianach remembered that very fondly, a day out with Daddy. It was a special memory of which she often spoke.'

After much discussion, the family returned to Scotland to scatter his ashes.

'In the end, we decided on the summit of [Cross Craigs] in Perthshire,' wrote Fianach. 'It was a beautiful tranquil place, where he had, over many years, enjoyed stalking. I remember that the sun suddenly emerged from behind the clouds as we scattered the ashes and said the Lord's Prayer.'[8]

That Cross Craigs overlooks both the trout-rich Loch Rannoch and the town of Aberfeldy, where her father had often watched Breadalbane Cricket Club during those long summer holidays, seems all the more appropriate.

History has been hard on Douglas Jardine, but Fianach would be delighted to see that the tide is at last beginning to turn. His portrait is in the Lord's Long Room, his cigar box in a case in the MCC Museum, while a stream of articles and books continue to examine and re-examine the legacy of what is still the most talked-about Test series in the history of the game. Even Shane Warne, that most Australian of Australians, has professed his admiration for a man who, in his words, had the 'courage to change the game's parameters.'[9] It is no less than he deserves.

'As a batsman he was upright and unbending, strong in defence and to the onside,' wrote Sir Neville Cardus on the news of his death. 'His hat was scrupulously straight. The fastest bowling could not hurry him. His batting, indeed, was like the man himself – calm, well-bred, not given to rhetoric, common-sensed, and imperturbable.'[10]

Good Scottish traits, he might have added. From India to England, Australia and beyond, Douglas Jardine never lost sight of that which defined him. A fine England captain – the finest of them all, perhaps – but always a Scot at heart.

9

From the Ashes

'After a man has a roof over his head and his bread and butter is fairly well assured and has a surplus, I think you will agree with me that it is only common sense that he should spend part of that surplus for the benefit of his native city.'[1]

The benevolent shadow of Arthur Kinmond Bell is cast long over the city of Perth. A man in whom business acumen was matched in equal measure by social conscience, Bell's establishment of the Gannochy Trust in 1937 was a truly remarkable gift from a proud Perthite to the city of his birth.

The family whisky company had prospered under AK's stewardship during the first part of the twentieth century, and with the effects of the Great Depression hitting hard, the businessman decided to embark on a series of altruistic ventures to benefit his fellow citizens. Amongst his early projects the Gannochy Housing Estate looms large to this day, and with the foundation of the Gannochy Trust five years before his death he ensured that his charitable works would live on well into the present century.

It is a legacy for which the city's cricketers have particular reason to be grateful, too, as Bell's lasting monument to his love of the game has safeguarded their future today. And as a new chapter in the history of Perthshire cricket begins to be written, a previous one is celebrated, too, as the story of Bell's friendship with the most celebrated player of them all is proudly remembered.

Founded in 1826, Perthshire, or Perth County, was one of Scotland's most formidable cricketing powers. Based at the historic North Inch, which would regularly draw four-figure crowds to the annual derby with Forfarshire, the 'Big County' was a founder member of the Scottish County Championship in 1902 and claimed its title no less than twenty times in the years between 1953 and 1978.

AK Bell was a more than adept player for the county side himself. In 1901 he appeared against the touring South Africans at the North Inch, scoring 21, and nine years later captained a team representing the Scottish Counties in a match against Yorkshire at the same venue.*

---

* The great Wilfred Rhodes, to whom Bell lost his wicket that day, was employed as Perthshire's professional in 1937. It was not the first time he had played club cricket in Scotland – Rhodes spent the summers of 1896 and 1897 at Gala Cricket Club in the Borders, for whom he took 169 wickets.

In a career which also took in appearances for Grange in Edinburgh, Bell's playing pedigree is further underlined by the century he scored for Wolfhill CC, another Perthshire team, at the age of fifty-five.

In an article which appeared on 27 July 1900, the day of the annual 'Battle of the Shires' between Perthshire and Forfarshire, the *Dundee Evening Post* gave its thoughts on AK's cricketing credentials.[2]

'AK Bell was for a number of years the captain of the team, and a dashing bat,' the column reads. 'While [he is] at the wicket the bowlers generally have a lively time, although, when occasion requires, he can be "dour" in true "barn-door" style.

'He has compiled some very good scores in his day, and this year has on several occasions been amongst the 60s. He is a fine [fielder], and a sure catch.'[3]

It was in keeping with his character that AK was most drawn towards the social benefits of the game, however, and as he encouraged participation in cricket he oversaw the design and construction of what remains one of the finest facilities in the whole of Scotland.

'There can't have been many people who had the resources to build their own cricket ground, but AK Bell's huge interest in the game led to him purchasing Kincarrathie Park in around 1924, a little before work on the Gannochy Housing Estate began nearby,' said Dr John Markland, Vice Chairman and Trustee of the Gannochy Trust. 'It is in a beautiful setting with some wonderful views over the hills to the north and west.'

Renamed Doo'cot Park,* the ground accommodates two cricket pitches within its borders, but it is the larch-clad pavilion which provides its most striking feature. Stone-built, with an octagonal pan-tiled roof and external wooden staircase leading up to a main room and balcony, the arts-and-crafts style building was awarded Grade B listed status in 1965.

The Doo'cot pavilion is one of Scottish cricket's most iconic sights, and in November 1934, nine years after work on the park had been completed, it received a particularly illustrious visitor.

In the early 1930s, Donald Bradman was at the peak of his powers. Statistically the finest batsman the world has yet seen, his Test average of 99.94 set a standard which no other player has come close to equalling. 'His contribution transcended sport,' wrote Matthew Engel. 'His exploits changed Australia's relationship to what used to be called the "mother country".'[4]

Quite how the very different worlds of Bradman and Bell came to coincide, though, is open to speculation.

'AK and his brother had been in Australia for quite long periods during the 1920s and '30s, but there is no evidence from his correspondence that he encountered Bradman while he was there,' said Dr Markland. 'There is, however, a photograph taken at the Gleneagles Hotel during the 1930 tour which opens up an interesting possibility.'

On 20 Sunday July – the rest day in the middle of the match at Hamilton Crescent – the tourists had unwound

---

* The new ground hosted its first match in July 1925 when AK Bell led an eleven drawn from local sides against the Oxford Authentics.

with a game of golf at the famous Perthshire course before their journey back to Glasgow for the resumption.

'The group photograph taken to mark the occasion has been very badly cropped, but in the front row is a very young Bradman and standing in the middle is someone that looks very much like AK Bell,' said Dr Markland. 'There is no way of guaranteeing that this is the case, but there is at least a chance that they met on that occasion.*

'What we know for certain, however, is that Donald and Jessie Bradman stayed with AK and Camilla Bell during his next visit here, in 1934.'

Much water had passed under the bridge since he was last in Scotland. Bodyline had been and gone, taking with it the careers of Douglas Jardine and Harold Larwood as MCC disassociated itself from its former captain. After weathering the storms which had raged Down Under, all were relieved that the first meeting between England and Australia since those troubled days had passed by free of dispute.

But not, however, of serious incident.

Bradman had suffered periodic bouts of illness throughout the summer and the lack of a conclusive diagnosis was to very nearly cost him his life. During late September the culprit, acute appendicitis, developed into post-operative peritonitis as Bradman endured days of pain and high temperatures battling an illness which at the time

---

* Whilst this premise is clearly plausible, the fact that the local newspapers made no reference to AK Bell's presence at Gleneagles is significant. It is quite possible, therefore, that the visit to Perth in 1934 was the first time that the two men had met – the Bradmans received many offers of hospitality from well-wishers as Donald recuperated, and it may simply be that AK's invitation was extended and accepted in this spirit. The absence of clear evidence either way, however, means that all theories will remain matters of conjecture.

commonly proved fatal. King George V asked to be kept informed of the cricketer's condition as, back in Australia, Jessie Bradman prepared to make the four-week voyage to her husband's bedside.

Gradually, though, Bradman's health improved, and by the time Jessie arrived in Dover on 28 October he was out of danger. Six months of convalescence lay ahead, however, and with foreign travel out of the question the reunited couple spent the next eight weeks taking an unscheduled holiday in the United Kingdom. And so it was that on 22 November the Bradmans travelled north to Kincarrathie House, the Bell's Gannochy residence.

Three photographs provide an overview of their visit. One depicts the two couples on the steps of Kincarrathie, whilst another pictures the foursome at the summit of nearby Kinnoull Hill, a portrait which was widely reproduced in the local newspapers.

It is the third image which is most striking, however, and all the more so because neither Donald nor AK is pictured within it. Instead, we see Mrs Bradman and Mrs Bell; Jessie glances right, her arms folded against the November air, while Camilla eyes something unseen to the left, both seemingly unaware that the camera shutter is about to fall.

And there, to the side, is the unmistakable pavilion staircase of Doo'cot Park.

Where Donald and AK were as their wives apparently pass the time in waiting for their return is unknown. It is safe to assume that they were nearby, but quite what the most celebrated batsman in the world was making of his visit to Doo'cot that day will have to remain a mystery.

A contemporary account of the Bradmans' stay does exist, however. Reproduced in part below, it adds some colourful detail to the story.

'Yesterday morning [Mr and Mrs Bradman] were astir early and shortly after ten o'clock were climbing the slopes of Kinnoull in the company of their hosts,' writes the *Perthshire Advertiser*'s 'Cover Point'. 'Two cameramen and myself came upon them on the crest.

'This was not quite the same Bradman who had been at Gleneagles four years ago. He was just a boy then. Now he has matured and the responsibilities which fall upon the big men in big cricket have left their mark on this young genius from Cootamundra. But while he looks more than his twenty-six years there is still an attractive boyishness about him. Believe it or not, Don is still shy.

'I knew better than to press the Champion, as the Australians put it, for his views on the MCC's ruling with regard to dangerous bowling. He hasn't any views meantime – for publication! But although talk on such controversial matters was taboo Mr Bradman was not loath to express appreciation of the beauties of Perthshire as revealed from Kinnoull's 500 feet. Nor was Mrs Bradman.

'As the party wound their way to the top they made several halts to survey new prospects unfolded by the twisting paths. Mr Bradman, who said earlier in the morning that he felt very fit, showed that he had fully recovered from his illness by taking several of the steeper inclines at a run – and one was irresistibly reminded of that familiar jog trot between the wickets. He wore an overcoat but Mrs Bradman chose to make the ascent without one. To her the trip into Scotland was a new experience, and one which she found delightful.

'Unfortunately for the sightseers the city was almost entirely screened by fog, but beyond was the sunlit vista of the Tay valley, with the snow-capped Grampians towering behind. On reaching the summit we found Mr and Mrs Bradman perched on a rock, gazing into a sea of mist, disappointed that one of the finest panoramas in the world was more or less completely obscured, but admiring the curious colour effects produced by the rays of the sun slanting through the banks of fog. Before making the descent photographs were taken with Mr and Mrs Bradman seated on the historic stone table and thoroughly entering into the spirit of the thing.

'Shortly after breakfast Mr and Mrs Bell accompanied their guests on a tour of the picturesque housing scheme at Gannochy, and an inspection was made of Doo'cot Park cricket pavilion. It was a proud day for Mr Tom Stead, the Doo'cot groundsman.

'Almost immediately after returning from Kinnoull Hill, Mr and Mrs Bradman left by road for the Lake District, having expressed themselves as delighted with their brief sojourn in Perth.

'Two very charming young people indeed.'[5]

The Don returned to Scotland for the last time as a player in 1948 when he led his 'Invincibles' to the final two victories of their unbeaten tour. A round of social engagements followed, including a trip to Balmoral to meet the Royal Family at the invitation of King George VI. There was to be no return to Doo'cot, though, just as there had been no further known contact between Bradman and Bell in the years leading up to AK's death in 1942.

That their meeting had left a fond impression, however, is made clear by its appearance within the pages of *Farewell To Cricket*, Bradman's post-retirement account of his life and career.

'Before setting out for Australia, my wife and I drove as far north as Edinburgh, where by now the moon had, in the shortening winter days, commenced to shed a useful as well as ornamental light round afternoon tea time,' he wrote.

'A short holiday was spent in Perth as the guests of Mr and Mrs AK Bell, a name famous in Scotland and elsewhere in connection with whisky. Not being a connoisseur [Bradman was teetotal] I offer no comment, but of AK I can speak affectionately.

'He was a true philanthropist and spared neither time nor money in endeavouring to advance cricket in Scotland.'[6]

It is a strange irony, then, that Doo'cot Park was destined to play a small hand in the eventual demise of AK Bell's beloved Perthshire. The facility had been created partly as a nursery to aid the development of players for the county side, but under the terms of Bell's bequest payment was dependent on the club remaining at its traditional home on the North Inch. A period of rapid decline both in the ground and the team, however, was to culminate in Perthshire being put into abeyance in February 2009.

Graham Ferguson had played for the team since his school days but, as its problems mounted, he was finally forced to yield to the inevitable.

'I was there until the end,' he said. 'There were about three or four of us desperately trying to keep things going, but ultimately we just didn't have enough players.

'The downward spiral had begun in 1993. There was a major flood that year which left all sorts of rubbish from the river over the Inch and us operating out of a couple of prefab huts for the whole season. It was horrendous and the standard of the pitch really started to deteriorate from that point on.

'We asked if we could come and play at Doo'cot Park but that was declined because of the terms of the trust, so eventually we had no other option but to put the club into abeyance.'

While Perthshire's last-ditch attempt to relocate to Doo'cot had failed, four other teams had already made their home on the Gannochy ground. The demise of the most famous name in the area, however, served as a bleak warning to Almond Valley, Strathearn, Mayfield and Northern as they continued to compete with each other for access to what was becoming an ever-smaller pool of players.

'After we lost Perthshire we all felt that we had to do something,' said Gordon McKinnie, then of Strathearn, 'but it took a long while for the clubs to reach a consensus that the best way forward was to look at a merger. There were always people who thought that combining our forces was a good idea, while, perfectly understandably, there were others who had their old club loyalties and wanted to keep things as they were.'

Two chastening experiences on the field focused minds further, however.

'Perthshire had been in the play-off to reach the National League in 2006,' said Graham. 'The first game had been rained off, and by the time the rearranged match came around our pro had had to go home and two of our other main players were unavailable. We went to play Glasgow Accies in Penicuik and got absolutely hammered. And, of course, while we were playing there were cricketers who played for the likes of Strathearn sitting in Perth watching the television, players who would have enhanced our team and made us much stronger that day.

'In 2010, in turn, Strathearn got to the play-off, and while they were being beaten by East Kilbride it was our guys sitting at home. So there was a gradual realisation that things could never go forward while the best players in the city were spread over four or five different clubs. It just didn't make sense. We started talking and pretty quickly there was agreement that something new was needed.'

And so, in 2011, Perth Doo'cot Cricket Club was born. A bringing together of five of the grand old names in Perthshire cricket – Perth County, Almond Valley, Strathearn, Mayfield and Northern – the new club has settled into life in the Strathmore and Perthshire Cricket Union and already collected its first trophy in the form of the 2013 Cricket Scotland Challenge Cup.

But perhaps most importantly as Perth Doo'cot looks to the future, its health on the field is being matched off it.

'We want to be much more than a cricket club that puts out a couple of elevens on a Saturday,' said Gordon. 'Our aim is to be a place in Perth where people want to come. We have a great facility and we don't want to have just half a dozen people hanging around it. We are not going to be amongst the top twenty playing sides in the country but we could become one of the top five in terms of how we do things to attract people into the ground.'

'From our perspective we are very interested in the community aspect of the new club and in particular how it relates to young people,' said Dr Markland. 'We have found that there has been much more of a coming together between where the club sees its future and where the Gannochy Trust is going.

'The Trust is very much focused on young people and on providing opportunities for everybody to participate in sport and we certainly feel that we're moving in the same direction. In the past, with all the different clubs, that was more difficult.'

'We feel that focusing on the all-round place of the club is the way forward, not just for Doo'cot but for cricket right across the country,' said Gordon. 'There might be fewer clubs in Scotland in the future but if that shift in thinking happens they'll be much stronger clubs.'

AK Bell would be proud to visit Doo'cot Park today. His spirit and vision lives on through the Gannochy Trust as well as in the new club which has so revitalised the game in his home city.

And if AK were to survey Perth Doo'cot's summer calendar, one particular event might catch his eye.

In 1959, Kincarrathie House, where Donald and Jessie Bradman had stayed a quarter of a century before, was bequeathed to the Gannochy Trust by Camilla Bell. AK Bell's house is now a residential care home for the elderly.

'We invite the residents of Kincarrathie to Doo'cot for a cricket tea during the summer,' said Gordon. 'We try to make it a special day, let them spend some time at the cricket. Properly spoil them a bit.'

It would undoubtedly bring a smile to his face.

10

Memories of Manjrekar

While AK Bell's bequest to Perthshire brought a number of famous names to the club over its final years – Justin Langer, Adam Gilchrist and Lal Rajput amongst them – few of the professionals that have played in Scotland can compare to Vijay Manjrekar. A thirteen-Test veteran by the time he joined Ferguslie Cricket Club in 1954, the influence of the Indian maestro is still felt in the town of Paisley today.

'I was about seven when he arrived at Meikleriggs,'* said Sandy Mathieson, whose involvement with Ferguslie has been virtually unbroken ever since. 'I just remember this beautiful, wristy style and the huge crowds that came to see him - four, maybe five thousand people. There was an Irishman, Paddy, who used to sit at the front gate and take sixpence in entrance money, although, being in Paisley, there were plenty of others watching as well. A cricket fan in this part of the world had a hole under their chin from looking over the fence!'

'They put canvas along the trees to try to stop people getting a free view,' added Stuart Black, who, like Sandy, extended his service to Ferguslie from the playing field to the committee room. 'There were thousands circling the boundary – three, four, five deep in places. Virtually every newspaper article of the time made specific mention of the numbers that were turning up to see Manjrekar.'

They were there to watch a player who had already prospered at the highest level. Having begun his Test career with a composed 48 against England in Calcutta (now Kolkata) in 1951, Manjrekar had provided a further demonstration of his blend of technique and temperament in an innings of 133 at Headingley the following year.† A fine cutter and hooker of the ball, he was, said *Wisden*, 'a conspicuously good player of fast bowling in an era when India had few of them.'[1]

---

* Ferguslie has played cricket at Meikleriggs since 1889, two years after its foundation as Ferguslie Threadworks Cricket Club. The philanthropic J & P Coats family, the internationally renowned thread makers, provided much support to the club in its early years, including the provision of the ground which remains its home.
† After coming in at 42 for three to face Fred Trueman and Alec Bedser, Manjrekar added a record 222 for the fourth wicket with captain Vijay Hazare.

On 24 April 1954, Manjrekar's introduction to Scottish cricket was similarly striking. On a cold, wintery day in Stenhousemuir, the twenty-two-year-old had given an immediate indication of his quality – and adaptability – in a fine innings of 72.

'It was reported that he took ten minutes to get off the mark as he got used to the pace of the wicket,' said Stuart, 'but from there he went on to play a terrific knock. This was at a time when it would be fair to say that if an amateur batsman got 20 or 30 it was considered a pretty good effort, but as the season went on Manjrekar was regularly scoring well in excess of that. He was consistently in the 40s and 50s and in one game was in the 90s, which was a big score in those days.'

Manjrekar's off-spin came to the fore the following week as he bowled through the innings to take five for 51 against Greenock, while the *Paisley Daily Express* highlighted a further aspect of his all-round game. 'A notable feature of the match,' the newspaper reported, 'was the brilliant fielding of Manjrekar, who was repeatedly applauded for his accurate returns and fast throwing-in. After several narrow escapes in the early part of the innings, the Greenock batsmen refused to run when the ball was near [him], much to the amusement of the spectators, who good-naturedly chaffed the batsmen.'[2]

Greenock's players would not be the last to demonstrate their respect for Manjrekar's ability. 'He was a great cover fielder, and always with his hands. He was never one to throw himself about the field.'

Joining the discussion is a true legend of cricket in the west of Scotland. Jack Kennedy's association with Ferguslie takes in more than half the years of its existence, stretching back as it does to his days as a junior cricketer in the 1940s. A former President of the Scottish Cricket Union who represented the club at every level, the greatest moment of his playing career came when he steered his team to victory in the Final of the Rowan Cup in 1960.* 'Senator Kennedy received the Democratic Party Presidential nomination in America,' declared the *Paisley Daily Express*, 'Jacky Kennedy got the freedom of Paisley's West-End.'[3] He has welcomed many professionals to Meikleriggs over the years, Balan Pandit, Reg Scarlett, Ashok Malhotra and Michael Hussey amongst them, but, for 'Wee Jack', it is Manjrekar who will always be king.

'He was one of those batsmen who always had so much time,' he said. 'He played very straight, and because he used his feet so well he could adjust extremely quickly. His shot was the cover-drive - just a push through the covers, all in the timing. It was immaculate.'

The disciplined precision of Manjrekar's game extended to other areas of his life as well.

'He was always impeccably turned out,' said Jack, 'and was a very traditional man. He lived up beside where the [Royal Alexandra] Hospital is now with an elderly couple who used to look after him, and when he walked down to the ground with his wife, she would always be walking ten yards behind him. And every so often he would stop and look over his shoulder, just to check that she wasn't getting

---

* Now known as the Murgitroyd Rowan Cup, the trophy is contested between the members of the Western District Cricket Union. Along with tournaments in the Caledonian and Borders regions as well as in the east of Scotland (where it is known as the Murgitroyd Masterton), the competition serves as the west of Scotland qualifier for Cricket Scotland's National T20 Finals Day. Jack is the last surviving member of the Ferguslie team which lifted the Rowan Cup for the first, and so far only, time.

any closer than she should. That was a very unusual thing to see, certainly in Paisley.'

Back on the field, Manjrekar's strong start to the season continued. He followed a superb innings of 95 against Uddingston on 12 June with another fine performance against Kelburne, his five wickets with the ball and elegance with the bat earning yet more praise from the local press. '[Although Manjrekar] had many scoring strokes negated by the slow outfield, his neat, wristy shots kept up the runs, mostly in well-placed singles,' reported the *Express*. '[His] innings of 40 … was full of delightful strokes correctly played and the spectators gave the young Indian hearty applause for a masterly display under difficult conditions.'[4]

But while it was Manjrekar who made the headlines, Ferguslie's team featured others of note, too. The victory over Kelburne added another chapter to the remarkable story of Jimmy Orr, whose four for 16 put the finishing touches onto the win which took Ferguslie clear at the top of the table. Jack's son Iain Kennedy, a former Scotland international who, along with his brothers Stuart and Graham formed a cornerstone of the Ferguslie team in the 1980s and 1990s, remembers with pleasure the hours he spent with a man who has since become part of cricketing folklore.

'Jimmy was born with polio,' he said. 'I can still picture the big boot he used to wear and his hands, he had the biggest hands. He wore callipers and was pretty much immobile, but he bowled left-arm spin which hardly anyone could read. We hear a lot these days about "mystery spinners" – well, Jimmy Orr was bowling mystery spin back in the '50s, '60s and '70s.

'Because of his disability he couldn't get sideways-on so he devised his own style, and with it he could make the ball turn either way with exactly the same action. He used to hipple in and deliver the ball face-on out of the front of his hand. You could hear it whirring through the air. It was mesmerising.'

For Iain, now Scotland's Chairman of Selectors, working with Orr at close quarters provided an invaluable education.

'When I was ten or eleven – he was in his sixties or seventies by this point – we used to sit together outside the pavilion. I'd be there with my bat and ball and he would bowl at me from eight or nine paces and say that if I could get a bat on one he'd buy me a Coke. I'd get nowhere near any of them, of course, so eventually he sat me down and explained that I needed to watch the direction of his fingers rather than at the ball coming towards me. Then he threw some more for me to try and catch, and I eventually got the hang of it.

'As a young boy, that was a great lesson which I carried into my playing career. I became very good at watching the bowler's hand because I properly understood the necessity of it.'

The full extent of the confusion felt by Orr's opponents, however, is laid bare by the record books. After taking seven wickets – five of them stumpings – against West of Scotland in 1944, Orr took sixty-eight wickets at 8.10 to see Ferguslie to the Second XI Championship two years later. In 1953 he was instrumental in bringing more silverware to Meikleriggs, his four for 13 helping Ferguslie defend a score of just 82 against Cartha to win its first Western Cup.

'In one game I remember taking three catches in the slips off his bowling, every single one of them a ricochet off the 'keeper's gloves,' said Sandy. 'There is no doubt that he would have represented Scotland had it not been for his disability - he couldn't field, so stood in the slips and batted with a runner.'

'Although,' said Jack, 'one very well-known cricketer once refused him that – the Reverend Jimmy Aitchison, of Kilmarnock.'

Few names resonate through the history of Scottish cricket more than that of James Aitchison. The 3,699 runs he scored from his sixty-nine capped appearances for Scotland included seven centuries, two of which came against the touring teams of South Africa and, in 1956, Australia, a performance which won him the admiration of opponents Richie Benaud, Keith Miller and Ray Lindwall. Comfortably the nation's leading run-scorer and cap-holder at the time of his retirement in 1963, the Church of Scotland minister played club cricket for Grange, Carlton and West of Scotland as well as for his beloved Kilmarnock, for whom he scored a remarkable 18,344 runs.

'I'll tell you a wee story about Jimmy Aitchison,' said Sandy. 'Our second XI was playing against West of Scotland, Jack here was the captain, and I took the first six wickets to leave them 28 for six. And this old boy came out wearing his pads and a pair of those old crocodile gloves, the green spiky ones, carrying an old bat. He took his guard, I bowled him an over and he spanked five of them straight past me for four. I turned to Jack and enquired as to who the …. this guy was?! And he said, very quietly: "That, son, is the Reverend James Aitchison!"

'We bowled them out for about 70 in the end, of which he got 28. But you were just in the presence of an absolute icon.'

'He did have an edge to him, though,' said Iain. 'Because Jimmy didn't have an injury which was caused in the game we needed the opposition to agree to him having a runner, which most did without any bother at all. But for a player, and a minister at that, to refuse him one in those circumstances maybe showed his character a wee bit. You'd hardly call it an example of the "spirit of the game".'

'But that's where cricket scores over a lot of sports, the characters you come across,' said Sandy. 'We could talk all day!'

Jimmy Orr continued to work his magic through the summer of 1954, but by its midway point his team had suffered a setback. A thumb injury had put Manjrekar onto the sidelines, and with the loss of captain Willie Somerville to a new job in England, too, the resilience of their title challenge was under examination for the first time. Momentum stayed with them, however, and with Manjrekar recovered and the team holding a narrow lead at the top of the table, Ferguslie travelled to Coatbridge knowing that victory over third-placed Drumpellier in the final match of the season would see them clinch the championship.

Should Ferguslie lose, there were two other teams waiting to take advantage. A defeat for the league leaders at Langloan would allow second-placed Greenock to overtake them with a win over bottom team Uddingston, while Drumpellier's hopes rested on the trickier combination of a victory at home and a favour from 'Uddy'. With the unpredictability of the weather adding a further variable to the mix, the destination of the crown was far from settled.

In the event, it was the least likely of the three scenarios which unfolded. Batting first but soon in trouble, Ferguslie only reached three figures thanks to the efforts of tail-enders Matt Peacock (36) and Jimmy Orr (10 not out),* and despite losing early wickets themselves in their chase of 103, Drumpellier stood firm to claim the victory and, in due course, the league championship. With Greenock's defeat at Uddingston confirmed, the Western District Cricket Union title returned to Coatbridge for the first time in thirty-one years.

For all the disappointment of its final day, it had still been a memorable season for Manjrekar, whose 577 runs at 39.70 and thity-eight wickets at 12.50 represented a more than respectable return from his injury-shortened campaign. 'The young Indian, although not accustomed to soft wickets, has performed excellently,' summarised the *Paisley Daily Express*.[5] His best, however, was yet to come.

Manjrekar began 1955 on international duty in Pakistan, but by April he was back at Meikleriggs for the start of his second spell in Scotland. He kicked off the season

---

* After slipping as he played his shot, Manjrekar was given out hit wicket for 15, his lowest score of the league campaign.

with a fifty against Greenock and a magnificent century against Clydesdale, while two seven-wicket hauls for Jimmy Orr spun Ferguslie to further wins over Ayr and Kilmarnock. Another half-century from Manjrekar saw Kelburne defeated, and after hitting 64 of Ferguslie's 208 for nine at Langloan, he and Orr shared eight wickets between them as the defending champions were bundled out for 105 in reply. The ghosts of the previous summer had been well and truly exorcised.

With two games remaining and Ferguslie clear at the top of the table, second-placed West of Scotland travelled to Meikleriggs in a last-ditch bid to close the gap between the two. Orr and Manjrekar, however, would once again emphasise the gulf that still remained. Orr was all but unplayable, his six-over return of five for 14 initiating the West's collapse from 56 for two to 75 all out, while another unbeaten fifty from Manjrekar anchored Ferguslie's gallop to the win and, as it turned out, the title. With rain washing out the season's final weekend, the twenty-three-year-old's match-winning boundary turned out to be the last act of both the summer and his two-year Ferguslie career. There could have been no more fitting way for him to sign off.

While Jimmy Orr finished with ninety wickets at 12.01, Vijay Manjrekar returned to India having completed the rare double of 1,500 runs and fifty wickets.* Two months later he was playing Test cricket again, lighting up India's home series against New Zealand with innings of 118 and 177, a score he would eventually surpass with an unbeaten

---

* Manjrekar scored a total of 1,669 runs at 66.8 in all competitions and took fifty-four wickets at 18.60.

189, his highest of all, against Ted Dexter's England in December 1961.

Although problems with his weight slowed him down in later years, Manjrekar's nimble footwork and natural ability remained, and against New Zealand in February 1965 he marked his final innings in Test cricket with his seventh Test hundred. While India never quite saw the full fruition of his early promise, his record of 3,208 runs at 39.12 in fifty-five matches, scored at a time in which the side was still finding its feet in the world game, represents a mightily impressive return nonetheless.

The future would see other professionals enjoy success at Ferguslie, amongst them Balan Pandit, who helped the club to a share of the title in 1959, and the popular Barbadian Adzil Holder, who, between the years 1965 and 1970, played an instrumental role in bringing two more championships to Meikleriggs as well as a first-ever Scottish Cup – then known as the Rothman's Quaich – in 1969. Sandy Mathieson, Stuart Black and Iain Kennedy were all part of the side which secured Ferguslie's second in 1983, while further triumphs in Scotland's premier knockout competition followed in 2005 and 2008.

But while the Ferguslie of today has struggled to reproduce the consistency of its earlier years, victory in the Western Premier Division in 2018 suggests that a new era of success may be on the way. And if ever further inspiration is required, the story of Vijay Manjrekar, Jimmy Orr and that *annus mirabilis* of 1955 will always be there to provide it.

11

THE HISTORY BOYS

Of all the tales of cricket in Scotland, there are none more joyous than that of Freuchie Cricket Club. The Fifers' momentous journey to Lord's and the final of the National Village Championship in 1985 turned the form book on its head as they became the first, and so far only, Scottish team to lift the prestigious Village Cup. 'The Skirl o' the Pipes Bowls Them Over at the Home of Cricket,' announced the following day's *Sydney Morning Herald* as news of Freuchie's success travelled far indeed.[1]

From his seat in the pavilion which now bears his name, Dave Christie smiles as he looks back on an achievement which may never be equalled. Now in his ninth decade, the cup-winning captain still lives in the village today, and as he tells me the story of Freuchie's journey from humble beginnings to national prominence it is clear that the passage of time has done nothing to diminish the pride he still feels in both his club and its success.

'When I first joined Freuchie as a thirteen-year-old, scoring the book for the second XI back in 1949, things were pretty much the same as they are today,' he began, 'first XI no problem, second XI struggling a bit to get players to make up the team. That's been the case with a lot of clubs over the years, always a wee bit of a struggle to put out a full second XI.

'In those days the club was only playing friendly cricket, and then almost always in Fife,' he went on. 'We didn't go "abroad" across the Tay or the Forth until about 1970, when we went to play a friendly in Arbroath. I remember that occasion well because the President of the time wouldn't allow us to play under the name of Freuchie Cricket Club. Tommy Henderson was our captain, so we played as Tommy Henderson's XI instead,' he chuckled.

'But the launch of the [National Village Championship] in 1972 gave us the kick up the backside we needed. We were just an ordinary team of ordinary guys but we decided to set ourselves the target of winning the Scottish section of the competition. The opposition was strong – St Boswells and Meigle, for example, both had very good teams – but by 1980 we had also joined Division Four of the East of Scotland Cricket Association, and with that as well as the Village Cup, the club really began to take off.'

Ably marshalled by PE teacher Terry Trewartha, Freuchie's training regime intensified as the ambition of its players grew stronger.

'We knew that if we wanted to compete with the best teams we had to become a far better fielding side,' said Dave, 'so we put a lot of work into that part of our game as well as the usual batting and bowling. As a result we lost the Scottish section only once in the 1980s and that was to Meigle, who, as I said, were an excellent side. I always thought they would be at Lord's before us, in fact, but in 1985, well, that was it.'

Nicknamed 'Dad's Army' in tribute to their forty-eight-year-old skipper, it was Freuchie's coolness under pressure which would ultimately see them home. Their passage through the early rounds of the competition was straightforward as both Dunlop and Rossie Priory were well beaten, and by restricting Breadalbane to 73 for seven in the semi-final another showdown with old rivals Meigle was secured. There, despite an early wobble – '[Freuchie] revel in shooting themselves in the foot, digging themselves into holes, and making life a thoroughly treacherous business,' vice-captain David Cowan* said later – Freuchie's 41-run win took them on to the Regional Final as Scottish Champions.[2] Mention of the elephant in the room was deliberately avoided, but the first leg of the road to Lord's had been safely negotiated.

Victories over Etherley and Cleator, the latter by only four runs, saw Freuchie into the quarter-finals of the main

---

* David Cowan would go on to win twenty-five caps for Scotland in the years between 1989 and 1997.

draw, where Oulton's collapse handed the Fifers a six-wicket home success. With Lord's now within touching distance the Scots were not to be denied as, on a cold, wet day in Fife, Freuchie's bowlers held their nerve to defend 117 against Billesdon to confirm their place in the Grand Final. Dad's Army, already in new territory, had broken its most significant ground of all. From its comparatively modest early ambitions, only Rowledge Cricket Club now stood between Freuchie and the Village Cup itself.

'Before 1985 we had always said that we just wanted to get to the final, no matter what happened after that,' said Dave, 'but the minute we won the semi all that changed. By the end of the night we were going there to win. We weren't about to be patsies to any English team.'

On 1 September, around 3,000 Scottish supporters – a thousand more than the entire population of the village – followed Pipe Major Alistair Pirnie and the kilt-clad squad through the Grace Gates and into Lord's. 'The crowd in attendance was, according to frequent visitors … greater than at many first-class county matches,' noted *The Scotsman*.[3] If the Home of Cricket had never seen anything quite like this tartan invasion before, it would soon bear witness to a game which more than matched the passion of its foot-soldiers.

After asking the Scots to bowl first, Rowledge captain Alan Prior watched David Cowan draw first blood for the Fifers as he claimed the wicket of Bob Simpson (6), and although Neil Dunbar and Tony Hook put on 41 for the second wicket, their progress was checked by some exceptional work from Freuchie in the field. Hook's dismissal for 28, bowled by the diminutive Niven McNaughton, was followed by two terrific pieces of fielding from Andy Crichton to run out both Dunbar (33) and Paul Offord (0) as Rowledge slipped from 56 for one to 74 for four.

Worse was to follow for the Surrey team as, spearheaded by the fast-medium of Terry Trewartha (four for 24) from the Pavilion End, Freuchie wrapped up the final five wickets for only 26 runs. 'It was well known that if you give a Scot "a bar of soap" they will bowl any side out,' wrote *The Cricketer International*'s Tony Huskinson. 'This time they did it with a dry ball and put on a display of fielding any side from any country would have been proud of.'[4]

'We were pleased at the halfway stage,' Niven McNaughton told Neil Drysdale, 'but we knew there was likely to be a ferocious response from their bowlers, and the atmosphere in the dressing room was one of relief that we had done ourselves justice, but combined with an awareness that our batsmen hadn't always set the heather on fire.'[5] Rowledge, all out for 134, had underwhelmed. The onus now, however, was on Freuchie's batsmen.

That all was still to play for soon became apparent as opening bowler Tony Field found a way through Mark Wilkie's defences, and when Andy Crichton (0), Alan Duncan (16) and George Wilson (14) followed, too, Freuchie's all-too-familiar fragility with the bat looked to have surrendered the advantage to their opponents. The big-hitting of David Cowan (16) and Stewart Irvine (24) released some of the tension, but the dismissal of both, Irvine straight after hitting a ball over the top of the Mound Stand – he later learned that Sir Garfield Sobers had been the only other batsman to have done so – set Scottish nerves on edge once more. When Trewartha followed, bowled by Jimmy Refford for 1, Freuchie's hopes, at 101 for seven, were in the balance.[6]

With 34 still required (and last man Niven McNaughton refusing to leave the sanctuary of the dressing room toilet) Dave Christie joined George Crichton in the middle. It was now Rowledge, however, which was feeling the pressure. 'We agreed we would run for anything feasible and test their mettle, because we had spotted the errors creeping into their fielding,' Freuchie's skipper recalled. 'It was still not cut and dried, but the balance of power had shifted to us and we knew that one boundary anywhere would seal it. Credit to Rowledge, they never ceased pestering and pounding us, but we had the scent of victory in our nostrils.'[7]

'They kept their heads, they kept their wickets, and they kept the score ticking along,' wrote Huskinson in a beautifully evocative passage. '"Dad" pushed a two through mid-wicket, Crichton two past extra-cover off the back foot. They took a single to mid-on and another to slip after a brilliant stop by Alan Prior. "Dad" charged like a champion. The tension mounted and even a psychiatrist started to bite her nails.'[8]

With seven balls remaining and only two runs needed, Christie charged once too often, however, and was run out for 11. Eight down and with only the terrified McNaughton to come – a batsman 'who batted at eleven purely because the rules forbade him from being number twelve' – the dismissal brought twenty-five-year-old Brian Christie to the crease.[9] Perhaps fittingly in this national celebration of the village game, the fate of Dad's Army would be decided by its captain's son.

A single from Crichton brought the scores level and the younger Christie onto strike, who watched the next delivery ricochet off his pads and run towards the boundary. The resulting pitch invasion was premature as the batsman had played no shot, however, leaving all to nervously resume their positions on the other side of the rope once more. Surrounded by opposition fielders but knowing that only survival was required, Christie blocked out the four remaining balls to see Freuchie's victory confirmed by number of wickets lost. 'It was,' summarised *The Scotsman*, 'a magnificent game of cricket and, in Scotland's bi-centenary year,* a fitting tribute to Freuchie and Scotland.'[10]

In front of 'a canvas of Scotsmen and Scotswomen going completely bonkers, united in joy', Dave Christie was presented with the trophy by Ben Brocklehurst of *The Cricketer International* magazine.[11] 'If anybody ever doubts whether Scotland can't be passionate about cricket,' the captain observed, 'they should have been there during that ceremony.'[12]

The celebrations continued long into the night as, back at the team hotel, a well-known face joined the party.

'England, who were halfway through an Ashes Test at The Oval, were also staying in the Westmorland Hotel, and Ian Botham came to the bar to have a drink with us after we'd won,' said Dave. 'He certainly sank a few. I had been presented with a gallon bottle of whisky and every time I passed by this big arm shot out with a glass

---

* The bi-centenary refers to a match played at Schaw Park, Alloa in September 1785, the first in Scotland for which records are available.

for a refill! And the next day, as we were nursing almighty hangovers, he took two brilliant slip catches as England won back the Ashes. How he could even see the ball I'll never know!'

'I have been to a few parties in my time, but few can compare with the Freuchie one,' Botham told Stephen McGinty in 2010. 'They made me feel really welcome. The publicity they got for their victory was amazing – they not only put Scottish cricket on the map, they put themselves on the cricket map throughout the world.'[13]

'The Village Cup was tremendous for us,' said Dave. 'It was a great thing not only for the village but for the whole of Scotland. Everyone got a buzz out of it, which, looking back, makes it all the more sad that today it's not what it was. In '85 the Scottish section had sixteen teams competing – last year there were five, which says a lot about what has happened in between. Not that long ago I was asked to write a list of all the Fife teams I had ever played against. Of the twenty-five I came up with, only five are left now. Huge changes.

'And it's so sad that as we sit here we're without two of our Lord's squad, George Wilson and Niven McNaughton, who have both passed away. They were great guys, real characters. When we had our twenty-fifth anniversary celebration, Nivvie turned up here on his mobility scooter! He lived in a wee cottage down in Ladybank and rode all the way from there to Freuchie, four miles down the A92. He could have been wiped out at any time! He was just that sort of guy.

'And Geordie Wilson, he had his own business before cancer took him. It's tragic that they have left us. It's an old bugger like me who should have been the first to go.'

Though time is moving on for many of Freuchie's Class of '85, the thirteen trees planted in the grounds of neighbouring Freuchie Primary School, one for each member of the Lord's squad, serve as a permanent reminder of that 'ordinary team of ordinary guys' which achieved the extraordinary. The same spirit which carried the majority of the village to Lord's for the final lives on today in a club which remains a representation of all that should be treasured in grassroots cricket: an institution which is truly at the heart of its community.

'Cricket has always been part of life here,' said Robbie Birrell, Freuchie's present-day President. 'Like everyone else we've had our share of ups and downs over the years, but we've always come through. The game is part of Freuchie. It is in our blood.'

12

The Captain and the Goalie

Across the Firth of Forth in the county of Midlothian, the cricketers of Penicuik have their own story to tell. The history of the town's cricket club stretches back to 1844, but it is the season of 2003 which is remembered with particular fondness.

For a Scottish side to have played a summer with one Test cricketer is hardly unusual. To have fielded two – as well as a celebrated international footballer – is surely unique. Penicuik began its season in the Scottish National

Cricket League with Australia's Graham Manou* in the team; by July, one of Pakistan's greatest-ever players was donning its maroon cap.

In contrast to the unsettled weather which claimed its first two matches, Penicuik's Division Two campaign had started brightly. Wins over Royal High Corstorphine, Edinburgh Academicals and Stewart's Melville Royal High (SMRH) had put the team into a strong position in the table, and with club professional Manou contributing a total of 154 runs from his position at number three, hopes were already high as the middle phase of the season arrived.

It brought with it, however, an unanticipated setback. On 15 June, Manou continued his promising start with an innings of 72 in the Scottish Cup tie at Uddingston, but in doing so he aggravated a rib injury which put him out for the next league match against Kelburne. Craig MacKellar's six for 9 maintained Penicuik's winning streak, but with Manou's absence subsequently confirmed as being for the remainder of the summer, a replacement for the popular Australian needed to be found as quickly as possible.

As Penicuik's representatives began to put out feelers, the presence of Rashid Latif's Pakistan in Glasgow† offered an intriguing line of enquiry. Former captain Inzamam-ul-Haq had given an interview in which he expressed interest in playing league cricket in England to improve his

---

* In the 2009 Ashes, Manou replaced Brad Haddin moments before the Edgbaston Test began when the Australian wicketkeeper broke a finger in the pre-game warm-up.
† Pakistan beat Scotland by one wicket in a fifty-over encounter at Hamilton Crescent on 7 June. The game formed part of their preparations for a three-match ODI series against England which began later in the month.

chances of an international recall, and Penicuik's initial approach centred on the potential availability of the prolific but mercurial batsman. His financial demands were considerable, however, and so, acting on a tip from local journalist Willie Dick, attention was turned towards a player whose future achievements would leave most others in the shade.

Then twenty-nine, Misbah-ul-Haq's international career was yet to take off, but his quality had been glimpsed in an ODI half-century made against Australia the year before. With the interest of both parties confirmed, negotiations were swiftly concluded, and at the conclusion of Pakistan's three-match series in England, Misbah returned to Scotland to throw his weight behind Penicuik's league campaign.

Speaking in May 2018 after a fundraising event organised by the charity Islamic Relief, Misbah told me about his time in Midlothian.

'Playing in Scotland taught me that I was perhaps a better bowler than a batsman, because I took a lot of wickets but didn't score a lot of runs!' he smiled. 'The conditions turned out to be very difficult for me, but it was a good experience to play against the ball when it was moving like that.

'I had a good time in Scotland. Penicuik is a small town and the people are very friendly. I enjoyed my time there very much.'

Misbah made his first appearance for Penicuik on 5 July in a home match against Stirling County. Although rain at Kirkhill caused the game to be abandoned at the halfway point, he took three for 39 with the ball, bowling a mixture of seam and cutters rather than the (albeit occasional) leg-spin for which he was known.

Pure pragmatism, as Penicuik opening batsman Michael Yan Hip explained, was behind his choice:

'If the weather is decent — and the summer of 2003 turned out to be a hot one — the middle of May to the end of June is when Scottish wickets are usually at their best,' he said. 'But by the time July comes around and pitches are starting to be reused, they tend to go very low and slow. These were the sort of wickets Misbah encountered that year.

'We had seen a similar situation before,' he continued. 'During the nineties another Pakistan Test cricketer, Rizwan-uz-Zaman, was with us for a season. He could bat for fun, just batted all day, and like Misbah he was a leg-spinner.

'Nowadays we are used to seeing leggies push the ball through quicker, but in Pakistan leg-spinners have often tended to bowl that wee bit slower, in the vein of somebody like Mushtaq Ahmed, for example. But Rizwan found that he couldn't get away with that here. Because the wickets were so slow, the league sloggers just smashed him round the park. Misbah started off bowling leggies, too, but switched to seam-up when he saw the situation.'

Misbah's five appearances for Penicuik brought him a total of eleven wickets at 18.80. 'He got through about sixty overs in total,' said wicketkeeper Graeme Leslie, 'and did an important job for us. He was always pretty accurate and tough to get away.'

'He was faster than your typical dibbly-dobbler,' agreed Michael. 'Graeme couldn't always stand up to him because the ball was coming on a bit quicker than you might expect. He bowled a heavy ball, hit the bat hard, and as he was coming in off only five paces or so it wasn't what the batsman expected at all.'

Although what had worked for Misbah with the ball was to conspire against him with the bat, he was not alone in being challenged by Scottish conditions.

'If you look at the records of a lot of overseas players over the years you will often see that the number of runs they scored in Scotland was pretty limited,' said Michael. 'They didn't know how to respond to Scottish pitches and dibbly-dobbler-type bowling, with the ball not coming on to the bat in the way they were used to.

'Twenty20 has changed that a bit now. Nowadays batsmen look to get their front leg out of the way and hit it anywhere between straight mid-on and mid-wicket. But at that time someone with a classical technique would often struggle against that type of bowling on this sort of wicket.'

'The conditions were totally different to what I was used to,' said Misbah. 'The wickets were very soft and there were some quality seam bowlers [of the type] we are not used to seeing at international level, especially in Asia and Pakistan where the pitches are very flat. It was surprising for me to see that in club cricket there could be such a difficulty to score runs.'

As his words imply, Misbah's batting turned out to be solid rather than spectacular. Having opened his account on 12 July with an unbeaten 37 in Penicuik's eight-wicket win at West Lothian – an innings which included 'a couple of on-drives which flew to the boundary like tracer bullets' in the words of Graeme Leslie – Misbah's home batting debut ended in disappointment as he was bowled for a duck by Falkland's Scott Sagar.

'In that game we eventually ground out a win after being in a spot of bother,' said Graeme. 'We were chasing a pretty modest total but [Sagar] had a bit of zip about him that day. There had been a lot of anticipation because Misbah was making his batting debut at Kirkhill, but he got a great ball which knocked his off-pole back and left us two wickets down with only 6 on the board.

'Willie Morton [formerly of Warwickshire and Scotland] and Ian Kirkhope played brilliantly to dig us out of it, though, and looking back it turned out to be the game which defined our season. It was a crucial win.'

*

As Misbah settled into life in the Scottish league, he was joined at Penicuik by another international sportsman of particular renown. Former Rangers and Scotland goalkeeper Andy Goram was in his second spell with the Midlothian side as he rekindled his cricketing career in the twilight of his footballing days.

Goram had played cricket for a variety of clubs in the Saddleworth League during his time at Oldham Athletic in the 1980s, and after his transfer to Hibernian he turned out for Penicuik before moving on to Kelso, West Lothian and Uddingston. A left-handed batsman and right-arm seam bowler, 'The Goalie' remains the only Scot to have played both a first-class cricket and full international football match for his country.

'Andy joined us in 1988 after signing for Hibs the year before,' said Michael Yan Hip. 'He was living in Bonnyrigg [six miles from Penicuik] and when he asked if anyone knew of somewhere he could play cricket, one of his teammates pointed him in our direction.

'He came along to a couple of pre-season nets and we could see straight away what a good player he was.'

'Andy was a fierce competitor,' said Graeme Leslie. 'He hit the ball very hard, bowled with a bit of intensity off around ten to fifteen paces and was one of the best gully fielders I have ever seen. His hands and agility were absolutely incredible.'

'He was a class act, no two ways about it,' agreed Penicuik President John Downie.* 'He had been on Lancashire's books as a junior and could easily have played cricket professionally had he not chosen football. Having him here was like having another pro. He was that good.'

Goram's first match for Penicuik saw him in dominant form as he got the better of a famous name of the future.

'Andy's debut was in a mid-week [Murgitroyd] Masterton Trophy match against Royal High School,' said Michael. 'Jimmy Adams, the future West Indies captain, was their overseas player that year and was making his debut too, if I remember rightly.

'It was May, early season, so the pitch was a bit damp and didn't have a lot of pace in it. I remember hitting the first ball of the match out of the ground and then Andy doing the same about five or six times. Jimmy was bowling slow left-arm stuff and The Goalie just kept smashing him into the houses on Kirkhill Road. He would either pick it off his feet or pull if it dropped short.

---

* John Downie also served as President of the newly restructured Cricket Scotland in 2001.

'That was Andy's introduction to Penicuik Cricket Club and Jimmy's to Scottish cricket!'

Goram's wholehearted approach to the two sports in his life led to an uneasy relationship between his respective teams, however.

'There was occasionally a little friction to smooth over with [Hibernian manager] Alex Miller,' said John Downie. 'I remember getting a particularly irate phone call from him after Andy had turned out for our seconds when he was supposed to be recovering from a broken finger. It was nothing, though. For someone like him an injury like that was just an irritation. The cricketer in him wanted to play.'

'I remember him telling Hibs the occasional white lie,' said Michael Yan Hip. 'When we were playing in the Indoor Sixes at Meadowbank, for example, he told Alex that we were playing with a soft ball when the ball we were actually using was harder than the real thing. If he'd then gone and broken something, goodness knows what would have happened.'

The conflict with Alex Miller began to come to a head in 1989 when Goram, with a move to Rangers on the cards, was selected to play for Scotland's cricketers against the touring Australians at Hamilton Crescent.

'The transfer speculation was at its height,' he wrote in his memoir, 'and Alex said, "You could break a finger in this cricket match and wreck the transfer. I don't want you to play. If you go and do this, I will fine you two weeks' wages."

'I was stunned and said, "Look, this means a lot to me. This chance will never come again. There are top county players in England who have never played against the Aussies." He was adamant, though, that my reward for playing for my country would be a fine of two weeks' wages. I took it.'[1]

That cricket provided Goram with a necessary release from the pressures of top-level football, however, was illustrated in 1990.

'Andy was away with Scotland at the World Cup [in Italy] but had been second choice to Jim Leighton throughout the tournament,' said John Downie, 'and when he found out that he wasn't going to be playing in Scotland's last match [against Brazil] either, he phoned me up from the team hotel to see if he could get a game of cricket instead. He flew back from the World Cup and played for us on the Saturday.

'But that same rebellious attitude could work against us sometimes,' he smiled. 'You could never be absolutely sure that he was going to turn up!'

Goram won the last of his five cricket caps for Scotland in June 1991, but his future ambitions were to be effectively ended by his seven-figure transfer to Rangers shortly afterwards. Ibrox manager Walter Smith, as fearful of potential injuries to his prize asset as Alex Miller had been, insisted that Goram concentrate fully on his primary career.

As his time in professional football drew to a close, however, Goram returned to cricket, playing seven games for Uddingston in 2002 before making his return to Penicuik the following year.

'Even though he hadn't really played for a number of years, it was clear that he still had the same natural talent,' said Graeme Leslie. 'In his second debut for us [against SMRH on 31 May] he ended up with four wickets and 20-odd runs. He got another four-fer against Hillhead [on 14 June] and a fifty in the return match with SMRH [on 9 August].''

But although he made only four league appearances for Penicuik that season, the larger-than-life Goram still left an impression.

'He was a good guy to have around the club,' said Michael Yan Hip. 'He liked being one of the lads and didn't want to be seen as anyone special. Even after he signed for Rangers he would still pop into the club for a drink from time to time.

'He never wanted to talk about football, which was interesting. He always wanted to talk about cricket, and he had plenty of stories of his time playing in the Saddleworth League with the likes of Ezra Moseley, Roger Harper and so on.

'But from a wider perspective his first spell with us was significant,' he continued. 'It coincided with us starting to believe that we could play a bit as opposed to being the Border League whipping boys which we always had been.

'Having him here gave the club a real lift and it definitely increased interest in cricket in general and in Penicuik Cricket Club in particular.'

*

Penicuik won three out of its final four matches in the 2003 season to pip Royal High Corstorphine to the Division Two title by less than a fifth of a percentage point.

'I was actually on the field when we won it,' said Graeme Leslie. 'We knew that we needed a certain amount of points to guarantee promotion but as I was walking out to bat we got wind that [leaders] Corstorphine had not secured their last batting point. We were just a couple of runs short of what we required and we got over the line. My contribution was a gritty nought not out of course!

'But it was a brilliant way to end what had been a great year. It was a strange season in many respects but a really memorable one. It was a proper team effort.'

After innings of 21 and 41 against Royal High Corstorphine and Edinburgh Academicals in his fourth and fifth games for the club, circumstances had dictated that Penicuik's final matches were played without their professional, however.

'I had to leave before the end of the season because Bangladesh was coming to Pakistan for a Test series,' said Misbah, 'and I was recalled to a training camp.'

'I saw him off at Waverley station,' said John Downie. 'We had a good chat and parted on good terms. I remember him saying that he was sorry he wasn't able to fulfil his potential for us.'

But although Misbah had felt the need to leave Scotland with an apology, the raw statistics of his time in Penicuik tell only part of the story.

For Kris Steel, making his first appearances in the Penicuik senior team as a thirteen-year-old, the opportunity to study an international batsman at close quarters was an unforgettable experience.

'Misbah was great to watch,' he said. 'I always remember one training session when he was receiving throw-downs from Pete Brannan, our Australian amateur. Well, I say throw-downs – Pete was actually bowling off a full run-up from the edge of the batting AstroTurf, letting fly at full pace about ten yards from the bat! I don't know how fast he was bowling but Misbah made it look easy.

'He was the type of player that made batting look completely effortless. He looked so confident, so in control and had so much time.'

One other training ground exploit has gone down in Penicuik folklore.

'We had the portable net pulled out onto the square and Misbah duly proceeded to hit the ball all over Kirkhill," remembers first XI captain Stephen Thomson. "He cleared the surrounding houses and goodness only knows where the balls were landing. It quickly became obvious that we had to stop as the locals could be in real danger!'

Stephen Green recalls that occasion well, too, and remembers Misbah as a modest, unaffected teammate.

'I found him to be a quiet, hard-working and highly intelligent man, someone who by his unassuming attitude you would never mark down as a future star,' he said. 'He was willing to spend time with everyone at the club, no matter what age or ability. So many of our junior players benefitted from his coaching and, speaking personally, I will always be grateful for the time and encouragement he gave to my son.'

Equally remembered is Misbah's off-field commitment to his game.

'I remember us playing in the final of the Masterton Trophy at Grange Loan,' said Kris Steel. 'The tournament doesn't allow professionals, so while the game was going on Misbah spent the best part of an hour doing laps of the ground. There must have been two or three hundred sitting on the boundary watching the match but there he was, doing lap after lap. It just showed the extent to which he would go to maintain his personal fitness.

'It was incredibly rewarding for me as a kid to get an insight into how a guy who had already played several times for his country operated on and off the field.'

'Because I was a fully-fledged [international] cricketer at that time and in line to play for Pakistan, it was very important for me to keep working hard on my fitness,' remembered Misbah. 'I used to practise the whole week and do extra fitness training if it rained. I would go to the ground and train myself up to the standard which you have to meet at international level.

'But I particularly enjoyed working with the youngsters at Penicuik,' he concluded. 'There were a lot at that time that I used to work with, batting and bowling to them. It was good. Working with young players has always been a pleasure.'

His stay in Penicuik may have been short, but Misbah's time is remembered with fondness as much for what he brought to the team off the field as his contribution on it. And it is those same qualities which have enshrined Misbah's place amongst the sporting greats of his country.

Humility. Understatement. Lack of fuss. Cautious where necessary, but dominant when needed. And a natural talent underpinned by a steely, unquenchable determination.

Essential factors in a true champion, one might say – and the essence of Misbah-ul-Haq.

13

Pushing the Boundaries

As old as the story of Scottish cricket is, there is one central part of its narrative which has been added only recently. The history of the women's game in Scotland is a surprisingly modern one, but with strides off the field now being matched by some striking performances on it, the country is at last showing that it is more than capable of making up for lost time.

While women have played cricket in Scotland for many years – St Leonards School for Girls* in St Andrews, for example, was a beacon of the game in the late nineteenth and early twentieth centuries† – there seems to have been little ambition in its earliest days to take it beyond what tended to be highly localised roots. 'Understandably, therefore, the standard was poor,' remarked Isabelle Duncan, 'and in 1978 a [Scottish] women's team touring Ireland [was] slaughtered by the women's clubs in South and North Leinster.'[1]

Those days have passed, however. With Scotland Women's age-group and 'A' teams supported by a two-division club league and regional representative series, the structure underpinning the national side is moving towards parity with that of the men's, and after rising to eleventh in the ICC rankings on the back of top-four finishes in both the fifty-over and T20 World Cup Global Qualifiers, a place amongst the top ten teams in the world is now in sight. And when that next stage in its journey is finally realised, Scottish cricket will raise a celebratory glass to the woman who in many ways started it all.

It is early in the season at New Williamfield, and as the coaching staff of Stirling County Cricket Club begin to

---

* In August 1932 at New Road, Worcester, seven of the Scotland XI which played England in the first-ever representative women's international were St Leonards alumni. The school was the alma mater of Wimbledon champion Kitty Godfree, who excelled at cricket in her schooldays, and was further renowned as a cradle of girls' lacrosse.

† One of the stand-out names from the early years of women's cricket, former pupil Betty Snowball played international squash and lacrosse for Scotland as well as ten Test matches for England, a tally which included the first seven to be played by women. In the fourth, against New Zealand in Christchurch in 1934, she scored 189 runs in 222 minutes to set a world record in the women's game which was not surpassed for over fifty years. It remains the highest score in Test cricket by an Englishwoman.

set up for the session of junior training to come – gatherings attended by a healthy number of girls these days – Kari Carswell is there to lend a hand. The development of grassroots cricket has always been close to her heart, but today, as she squeezes a meeting with me into her visit to her old stomping ground from her new home in New Zealand, it is Kari's contribution to the wider advancement of the women's game which is the focus.

When the history of Scottish cricket comes to be written, Kari is sure to be amongst its most significant figures.[*] As player, captain and coach she created a culture where none had existed, instilling a desire to improve and succeed which remains at the heart of the national team today. Others played their part, as Kari herself is quick to point out, but it is hard to imagine that Scottish women's cricket would have reached the point it has without her.

'I've been very lucky in a lot of ways,' she began. 'Lucky in that I had two older brothers who were into cricket, lucky that I spent my school life at Dollar Academy and lucky in how it was that I started playing in the first place. Although I'd always played a bit in the back yard with my brothers, cricket wasn't a game that was available to girls when I was at school. For us it was a choice of either athletics or tennis, neither of which I was either interested in or any good at.

'But when I was in Primary 5 [around nine years old], I tagged along to a summer camp at Stirling County which my brother Gav was booked on,' she continued. 'I was sitting at the side, really bored, when one of the coaches came over and asked if I wanted to join in. And that was

---

[*] Kari played under her maiden name of Anderson throughout her career.

it. I asked at school if I was allowed to play cricket instead, they let me give it a go, and it sort of snowballed from there.

'It was never my intention to be a cricketer – I played district level hockey when I was at school and always thought of myself as more of a hockey player – but in my last couple of years at Dollar, cricket took over. Someone was looking down on me I think!'

With no pathway at either local or national level for female cricketers, however, it was a predominantly male world into which she entered.

'There were no women's teams,' said Kari. 'I played age-group cricket at school and age-group stuff at Stirling, all with the boys. Kathryn White was at Stirling as well which was pretty cool, having another girl there, but that was very rare. I can't think of an occasion when we played against another female.

'It was tough, but it made you tough. We used to get ripped, but it made us both a lot stronger as a result.'

Four years her senior, Kathryn White had already played several seasons at Stirling County by the time Kari arrived. Still a destructive batter in both the club and regional game, she now plays a major role in the development of the next generation of female talent as assistant coach and manager of the national Under 17s.

'I had been introduced to cricket at primary school by Raymond Bond, who coached at Stirling County and was also employed as a Development Officer by the local council,' said Kathryn. 'I was fortunate. I got a chance, enjoyed it and the cricket ground happened to be right next door to my school so it was easy to get to. I did the usual round of Kwik Cricket tournaments, one of them sponsored by Wrigley's as I remember. We got a huge box of chewing gum when we won. Imagine that these days!' she laughed.

'I was in the Under 18s at Stirling when I first met Kari. Our careers kind of went along together from that point onwards; for a long time, though, it was pretty much the two of us.'

Although it would not be until 1999 that the idea of a national side began to take shape, a women's team did at least exist in Edinburgh. Dublin-born Linda Spence[*] had been the driving force behind its formation at Grange in the middle of the decade, and after accepting invitations to join, both Kari and Kathryn were given their first chance to play cricket in an all-female environment.

'We used to compete in the Northumberland League,' said Kari, 'and we were good, we used to win it pretty much every year. It was a really good experience, jumping in the car at seven o'clock on a Sunday morning, playing the game then coming home, but what it showed us most of all was that we weren't alone. I would have been about sixteen or seventeen, pretty young but nothing like the five- or six-year-olds who are coming into the game now. They play alongside other girls right from the start, but for us to see that there were other women out there who played cricket too was a pretty big thing.'

Linda Spence brought together a dedicated group of players, who, by the end of the decade, formed the core of Scotland's first national women's team.

---

[*] Linda Spence, who would go on to make sixteen capped appearances for Scotland Women, became the side's first captain in 2001.

'Linda has to take a lot of credit,' said Kari. 'She was the one who went knocking on doors to say that we wanted a national team. There was no big fanfare about it – it was a case of, okay then, on you go.

'But we are talking about a very, very small pool of players here. We were building towards the 2001 European Championship in England, but, basically, if you were a woman who played cricket in Scotland, you were in. There was nothing even approaching a pathway to get there.

'At one selection meeting we had a total of fourteen players to choose from. Not many would have got near the national squad today, never mind the team, but it's where we were. If you could hold a bat, you were in. If you were committed, you were in.'

Kari's own dedication to Scotland's cause was plain from the very start. Her performances in the Northumberland League had led to an invitation to trial for England, but, when faced with the choice as to where her ultimate ambitions lay, there was only ever going to be one outcome.

'At the same time as we were getting ready for that first European Championship, I was involved in the England squad,' said Kari. 'I'd just moved up to their Under 19s having played a series against Holland for the Under 17s,[*] but at that point I made the decision that I wanted to play for Scotland in the future. I've always been passionate about trying to develop the game up here and so that was what I decided to do.'

---

[*] Kari scored 54 runs at 18.00 in England Under 17's three-match series against the Netherlands in August 2000. Her teammates included Isa Guha, Ebony Rainford-Brent and Lydia Greenway.

With Kari fully on board, the new team began to take shape. Working alongside Linda Spence was coach Clarence Parfitt, who made a significant contribution to Scottish cricket after his permanent move to the country from Bermuda in 1984. His impact on the side would be considerable, even though his initial appointment was as much about practicality as suitability.

'Clarence was working for Cricket Scotland as a Development Officer and we needed a coach, simple as that,' said Kari. 'I don't know if he was the only one willing to do it! But he was certainly that. He was very dedicated and enthusiastic.

'He had a tough job. In the early days we never really got together that much as a team, maybe once a month or something like that. We'd work in the nets and talk through our game-plans and so on, but boy, we were pretty raw. We were basically just people who played cricket and happened to know that there was a women's squad.

'But Clarence did a really good job for us,' she continued. 'His role as Development Officer covered the north of Scotland, so as he went round the clubs and schools up there he had the perfect opportunity to scout out new talent, which he did on a regular basis.'

After meeting success in their first competitive outings – a seven-wicket win over Northumberland was followed by a ten-wicket victory over Cumbria in June 2000 – Scotland's women prepared for the European Championship with two matches against major county opposition the following summer. Kari's return of four for 18 in the 28-run win over Durham was followed by an innings of 70 against Yorkshire as Scotland, chasing 148, claimed its biggest scalp so far. Her stay at the crease was ended by future World Cup-winner Katherine Brunt, but it had been enough to set up a four-wicket victory with two balls to spare.

There was to be no repeat in the European Championship itself, however, as heavy defeats to England, Ireland and the Netherlands ensured that Scotland's first taste of international competition would be delivered by way of a wooden spoon.

'Oh we got pumped!' chuckled Kathryn. 'But we took from it what we could and we moved on.

'In sport you have to lose to discover the things that you need to know,' she continued. 'Beforehand we had prepared as best we could, but having actually been there and put ourselves up against that standard of team, we had something concrete to take away and use. It was a beginning.'

The following year brought another as, at the age of nineteen, Kari succeeded Linda Spence to the national captaincy. Her first major assignment came in 2003 in the form of the International Women's Cricket Trophy in the Netherlands, where Scotland secured fifth place in the six-team competition with a 57-run win over Japan. With 112 runs at 22.40, Kari finished the tournament as its second-highest run-scorer. Victories over European opposition remained elusive, however, and in 2005 Scotland finished bottom of the European Championship again after defeats to Ireland, the Netherlands, Wales and an England Development XI containing Sarah Taylor and Laura Marsh.

Although the team had come up short against their nearest neighbours, Scotland's match against Ireland had at least been significant in another way. The game marked the international debut of fourteen-year-old Abbi Aitken-Drummond, who would go on to play a significant role of her own in the future progression of the side. Back in 2005, though, it was very much the captain who was setting the tone both on and off the field.

'I was in total awe of Kari and, to be honest, a bit intimidated by her as well,' said Abbi. 'She was such a good cricketer. You didn't want to bowl at her and you didn't want to face her because she had it all.

'But even though she was by far and away the best player in the team, she wasn't in-your-face about it or vocal in the sense of being one of its big characters. She did her talking through her cricket, and she had the absolute respect of everyone as a result. It's a bit of a cliché, but she genuinely led us by example.'

When it comes to self-appraisal, however, Kari is somewhat more down-to-earth.

'I was dull as,' she said. 'There was nothing flamboyant about me at all. But I knew my game. Working out what you can and can't do as a cricketer is so important. I was never going to hit sixes like Kathryn, for example – if I was going to get runs I knew I was going to have to run hard between the wickets for ones and twos and hit the odd ball for four when I could. But it took years to figure that out and then be happy with it, because I always wondered why I couldn't do all those other things as well.

'In the end, though, it was about what was important to me. I used to get frustrated at getting out, so I tried to bat for as long as possible instead. I'd have been really good if we'd played a Test match, I reckon. I'd have been quite content to bat all day.'

'Kari was the absolute backbone of the team,' said Abbi, 'but, looking back, it must have been tough for her. We would go seasons without winning a game, and to have had the cricketing ability she did but not get the results she deserved must have been really hard. She hit so many fifties, a couple of hundreds, and nine times out of ten they were in a losing cause. It says so much about her that she carried on doing what she did all the same.'

Progress was being made, however. In addition to her work as national captain Kari oversaw the launch of Scotland's first age-group team, and in March 2007 she was given the opportunity to spread the gospel of women's cricket still further when she was appointed to the role of Community Development Manager at Cricket Scotland.*

'For the national team to be viable we had to get more people playing the game,' said Kari. 'We had a Scotland team, which was great, but we had nothing at all supporting it. That had to change.

'Before I started at Cricket Scotland I had introduced a Scotland Under 17s,' she went on. 'I remember speaking to [Head of Cricket] Andy Tennant at the time and saying that we needed to be really careful, that if we didn't have something feeding into the senior squad then we weren't going to have a senior squad. As I remember we put something on the website asking for people that wanted to play to get in touch, and we got decent numbers in response.

---

* In August 2011, Kari became Cricket Scotland's first Girls and Women's Manager.

'But, again, if you played cricket you were a shoo-in, there were no trials or anything like that. We got involved in the Under 17 County Championship to get some regular games, and we took some pretty heavy beatings. But it gave us the opportunity to play, which was the only way we were going to learn. You can look a million dollars in the nets, but if you can't hit a gap in the field or bowl at the stumps you've got absolutely no chance. And that was what it was all about, getting in as many games as we possibly could.

'So when I got the role at Cricket Scotland my immediate focus was on schools' cricket,' she continued. 'Rightly or wrongly I started with the secondary schools and worked my way down to the primaries, just trying to create ways for more girls to play cricket. And then along with that it was trying to get as many clubs as possible to start women's teams.

'It was tough, you were up against a lot of ingrained attitudes, and I always remember thinking that now I'd been given this role, I'd better start by getting my own club on board. They said, on you go, you do it. So I did. But once we had one or two it got a bit of momentum going, we could have a bit of a league and a Scottish Cup competition. There were only four or five teams in it, but it was a collection of females playing cricket, and that was a huge thing.'

The sands were beginning to shift on the field, too. Scotland – now with Leigh Kasperek in the side – beat Cumbria, Northumberland and Durham to win Group Four of the ECB Women's County Challenge Cup in 2007, while Kari's unbeaten 114 against Northumberland set the newly styled Wildcats on their way to the Division Five title in their first season in the LV Women's County Championship in 2008. Restructuring took Scotland into Division Three for 2009, where four more wins saw the team finish above both Hampshire and Derbyshire in a creditable fourth place.

Kari's influence on the direction of the team was strengthened further by her appointment to the role of its player-coach in November 2010. A number of experienced players moved into the frame to replace her as captain, but Kari's eventual choice was in favour of one of the youngest members of the group.

'When Kari became coach there was obviously a lot of talk about who was going to be the new captain,' said Abbi Aitken-Drummond, 'but my name was never mentioned. I was nineteen at the time and had only been in the side for five years, which, when you consider that we played only four or five games a season in the County Championship, wasn't that long at all.

'It had never even crossed my mind, so when Kari took me to one side and asked what I thought about being the next captain, I was absolutely stunned. I just remember looking at her and saying "no way, absolutely not, there's no way I can do that" in typical me fashion, highlighting all the negatives and all the things that I thought I couldn't do.

'But in that calm way she had she assured me that she was continuing to play, that she knew I was inexperienced but that I had a really good relationship with the girls and that she would be there to guide me into the role at a pace I would be comfortable with. It would be fair to say that for the next season and maybe the one after that, Kari captained me. I was the voice, but Kari was a big part of the decision-making process.

'I owe her a lot,' she continued. 'Kari passed on everything she could to me, and I wouldn't have been anything like the captain I became without her.'

Once installed as coach, Kari set about addressing an area of the Wildcats' game which was still causing concern.

'I took over at a time when, to be honest, we were scared, and our run-rate was really poor as a result,' she said. 'How do you change that? You go out and play cricket. Hit the ball. If they're too fast for you, they're too fast for you. Just go and get better. That was something I always thought I could change, to make people better and believe in their skills. If you're not good enough then how do you improve? You go away and practise. That's life.

'My philosophy as a coach is no different to my approach as a player,' she continued. 'Don't try and do the things you can't. As soon as you come to terms with that you'll be much more content, and it's much less frustrating for the coach who is, after all, trying to build their team around the skills of the players they have in front of them.

'If your game is hitting sixes and fours, go and hit sixes and fours. The batter's job is to score runs, and I'm not going to scream and shout if it goes wrong. It's when somebody does something that they're not good at or they've not practised, that's when I get grumpy.

'Coaches used to say to me that if you bat your fifty overs you'll win games of cricket,' she went on, 'and that used to frustrate the hell out of me because, no, you don't actually. And we used to do that. We did that for years and years, batted our fifty overs, scored 120 or 130 then got beaten inside twenty.

'Cricket is about making runs. Try and get to 200 as quickly as you can and look on anything after that as a bonus. Take that mentality to the crease and you'll be all right. Bowling – just aim for those three stumps. Make the batter make a choice. Dead easy. And then catch it as well. Simple!' she laughed.

The Carswell/Aitken-Drummond partnership got off to a memorable start when, on 15 August 15 2011, Scotland's women recorded their first-ever win over Ireland. In the first match of the Women's European Twenty20 Championship in Utrecht, the Irish were dismissed for 72, and although Scotland slipped from 49 for three to 58 for six in reply, Fiona Urquhart and Sahar Aslam held their nerve to guide the team to victory off the final ball of the match. The Netherlands brought the Scots back to earth later in the day, but the significance of Scotland's achievement against a side which had always held the upper hand against them could not be underestimated.

The extent of the national side's progress was further illustrated in 2013. Although the team had failed to advance to the final stages of the Women's World T20 Qualifier, Scotland provided warm-up opposition for Canada and Thailand as they prepared for the tournament with four games in Dublin. Both were beaten twice-over, and with Division Three of the Royal London Women's One-Day Cup and a seven-wicket win over the Netherlands secured in 2014, too, Scotland was showing both competitiveness and consistency for the first time in its short history.

In 2015, Abbi Aitken-Drummond's team joined Ireland and the Netherlands in the ICC Women's World T20 Global Qualifier in Thailand. An extra place in the tournament had been awarded to Europe after off-field issues led to the cancellation of the ICC Americas Women's Championship the year before. Scotland, so long in the shadow of its neighbours, had been given its biggest chance of all.

On 28 November, Scotland began its Group A campaign in Bangkok with an emphatic eight-wicket win over Papua New Guinea. Defeat to top-ten team Bangladesh followed the next day, but, in the final group match on 1 December, Kari Carswell (two for 13) and Kirstie Gordon (two for 17) sealed a semi-final berth at the expense of the host nation. In their first appearance at a global tournament, the Scots were one win away from World Cup qualification.

Although there was to be no fairy-tale ending – a seven-wicket defeat to Ireland was followed by a penultimate-ball loss to Zimbabwe in the third place play-off – Scotland's arrival onto the world stage was complete. In July 2016, the national side booked its place at the fifty-over World Cup Global Qualifier in Sri Lanka with a three-nil whitewash of the Netherlands in Essex. Nearly fifteen years after their rivalry began with a run of twelve straight defeats to the Dutch, Scotland had turned the tables in emphatic style.

For Kari, though, it was the beginning of the final chapter of her Scotland career. At the start of 2016 she had called time on her five-year reign as national coach, and, looking ahead, she privately decided that the tournament in Sri Lanka would be her last. The 'old guard' was moving on – Kathryn White had already announced her international retirement, while Fiona Urquhart would soon follow. Incoming coach Steve Knox and, in due course, a new captain in Kathryn Bryce would be tasked with steering Scotland's women through the next stage of their journey.

Kari signed off with 111 runs at 27.75, a tally which included a half-century in Scotland's opening game against South Africa. Her final match, against Pakistan at the Colombo Cricket Ground on 13 February, was her 152nd for her country. The tributes which followed came from across the cricketing world.

'I had some outstanding performances as a player, but they're not the things I really remember,' reflected Kari. 'It's the funny things that happen: the laughs with your teammates, someone taking a sensational one-handed grab, the dropped catches that were dollies that you joke about in the years to come. Getting so close to the World Cup in Thailand was a massive highlight for me, just seeing how that squad had evolved to the point where we genuinely believed that we were going to make it. We were playing some really good cricket and there was such a good vibe in that squad –Scholesy [Rachel Scholes], Fi Urquhart, Abbi, Annette [Aitken-Drummond], Ollie Rae, Abtaha [Maqsood], Jacko [Lorna Jack], Sarah and Kathryn Bryce, Sam [Haggo], Katie McGill, Kirstie Gordon, Liz Priddle. We had a really good go and came up just short in the semi.

'The centuries, the five-fers, they were nice at the time, but you don't really remember them. Back at the start, whenever I scored runs we tended to lose, so in the end they didn't really mean a lot anyway. But seeing the girls come through and do well and the team get to where it did from where we started back in '99 – now, that was satisfying.'

Although life today revolves around her role as Female Pathway Manager at the Northern Districts Cricket Association in New Zealand, Kari's interest in the Scottish game is just as keen as ever.

'As I look around Scotland now, I see a really promising picture,' she said. 'More and more clubs are running women's teams, and cricket as a sport is on the up as a result. The old challenges will be there for a while yet, but there are loads of positives going on in Scottish cricket right now and it's great to see.

'You can't underestimate the benefits of proper structures and pathways,' she continued. 'You can't just deal with the here and now. It's a long-term game, and you always have to look to the future. That was something I cared about a lot in my role at Cricket Scotland, and it's still at the centre of what I do today.

'But I have to applaud what Cricket Scotland has done. They're always looking to innovate, and because of that I'm sure they'll carry on going from strength to strength in the future. Women's cricket is in a much better place than it was when I started my career, that's for sure.

'It was an interesting journey, and great fun along the way. The friends I've made are friends for life, and I have some incredible memories to look back on. I wouldn't swap that for anything.'

14

The Generation Game

On the road from Perth to Forfar, in the agricultural heartland of Scotland, lies the little village of Meigle. Crucible of early Christianity, a capital for the Pictish kings of the Middle Ages and, so legend has it, the final resting place of King Arthur's Guinevere, it is a community with a colourful past that can be traced back over many centuries. And thanks to Meigle Cricket Club, established in 1876, there is an eminent heritage on the cricket field which can be added to its story, too.

Family ties run deep and strong in this part of the world. A glance through Meigle's Roll of Honour sees many names recur, with Scott, Laing, Walton and Pattullo just a few of those inked into the history of cricket in the village.

There is one other, though, which persistently catches the eye.

The Drummond family name is woven through the fabric of the club. Beginning with Duncan and Jim Drummond in the early 1930s, through their younger brother Peter (Mitchell) and his son Peter (Charles James) and on to his sons Peter (James) and Gordon and daughter Annette, the family's association with Meigle's black and gold has spanned the best part of a century.

The three members of its youngest generation have enjoyed distinguished careers both in the village and beyond: Gordon and Annette won international honours with Scotland, while wicketkeeper-batsman Peter is still adding to the numerous awards he has collected at both club and regional level. But for each of them it is the interaction between family, club and community which has provided the greatest influence; in Meigle, as in so many other places across Scotland, it is there that the true measure of Scottish cricket is to be found.

'Cricket was a natural part of life when we were growing up,' said Peter. 'We lived right beside Victory Park [home of Meigle CC] and basically that's where we would spend our summer. It's where things started for all of us.'

'Sometimes when we finished school we didn't bother going home, we just went straight to the park,' said younger brother Gordon. 'Mum ran the tennis team, so we would play tennis, badminton and hockey as well as cricket and football. Everyone did. There's a real cohesive spirit within Meigle, and for us as kids that showed itself through sport.'

The example of their grandfather provided further inspiration. A prolific all-rounder who made his first XI debut as a fifteen-year-old in 1937, Peter M Drummond won the Laing-Ovenstone Memorial Trophy for the Strathmore Union's top wicket-taker in both 1951 and 1953. He went on to hold a variety of committee posts at Meigle, including President and Honorary President, before his passing in December 2016 at the age of ninety-five.

'I never saw Grandad play but I've heard so many fantastic things about him,' said Annette. 'People talk about him as being this incredible cricketer and he was so passionate about it. Any time you went round he would be in the conservatory because Granny had chucked him out of the living room and he would have his massive jigsaw puzzle out and the cricket on the television.

'That's just what he did and it kind of transferred to our household as well. Cricket is what we would talk about round the dinner table.'

'As well as Meigle, Grandad played for Perthshire, which in those days was a select team,' said Peter. 'They had a core of gentlemen which they would supplement with the best players from nearby, so it was quite an honour for him to be chosen and he was very proud of it. But although he had stopped playing by the time I took up the game, his love of cricket was a real spur to us all.'

His son Peter CJ Drummond was also fifteen when he made his debut for Meigle's first team. A member of three title-winning sides, his enthusiasm for the game provided further encouragement to his young family.

'When I was younger our weekends would consist of packing a picnic and going off to watch Dad play somewhere,' said Annette. 'Every other weekend was a wee trip away so it was quite exciting.'

'I took over the scoring when I was about nine or ten, which was my Dad's way of spending quality time with us at the weekend!' smiled Peter. 'But we would always make sure our kit was in the back of the car just in case one of us needed to jump onto the field at some point.'

'I loved watching Dad play because even though he was a bit of a slogger, at least towards the end of his career, he was always exciting to watch,' said Annette. 'One of my best memories is of batting alongside him when he ended up scoring a hundred. He'd played maybe twice all season but he just started smashing it. You could see that he was in form and totally loving it. Not many daughters get to play sport alongside their Dad, so it was pretty special.'

After rising through the ranks of junior cricket, Gordon and Annette became Meigle's third and fourth representatives to play for Scotland, with former captain Gordon winning 117 caps before his retirement from the international game in 2013. Today he continues to shape the future of Scottish cricket through his role as Cricket Scotland's Performance Pathway Manager.

'Through my youth I played a bit of age-group cricket for Scotland,' he said. 'Skill-wise I was okay and I had a bit of physical presence as well, but most of all I inherited a really positive attitude from my parents which always stood me in good stead.

'Because I was involved in coaching as well [Gordon studied Sport and Exercise Science at Napier University], I was able to support my own learning and development. I knew that I was never going to be an out-and-out fast bowler, so I worked really hard on making the most of the skills I had.'

A bowling all-rounder, Gordon made his senior debut for Scotland in the Friends Provident Trophy in June 2007.

'It all came about very quickly,' he remembered. 'I'd been doing well for the 'A' team, got lucky with injuries and before I knew it I was in the team to play Warwickshire. I got a phone call on the Saturday and was playing on the Sunday.'

Scotland competed in the ECB's limited-overs competition as the Scottish Saltires until restructuring in 2013 saw its number of participants reduced to include the English counties only. The exposure to top-level cricket did much to benefit the Scottish game, however, and although results were mixed, the Saltires could still look back on some notable scalps.

'One game I remember very well was at Old Trafford [on 6 May 2008],' said Gordon. 'Lancashire had a formidable team at that time, the likes of Andrew Flintoff, Stuart Law, Mohammad Yousuf, Faf du Plessis and so on. Flintoff was in his pomp. [Saltires' overseas professional] Ed Cowan came off having scored 41 off a hundred-odd balls and told us that he couldn't get anywhere near him!'

As the game unfolded, advantage would swing first one way then the other. Chasing 155, Lancashire was soon in trouble as Dewald Nel (three for 26), John Blain (two for 22) and Craig Wright (two for 34) combined to reduce them to 44 for seven, but with Kyle Hogg and Luke Sutton hitting back with a partnership of 71, it looked like the home team had done enough to claim most unlikely of comeback victories. For Gordon, however, the match was to take an eventful turn.

'Hogg hit one up in the air, and as I tried to get to it I tore my hamstring,' he said. 'With the game at the stage it was, though, I couldn't go off. They needed 10 off the last over, we needed one wicket, and [Saltires captain] Fraser Watts asked me to bowl. I was only able to walk up, but I kept firing in yorkers and somehow we got over the line by two.

'It was a really memorable victory because it was such a strong team that we had played against. We'd only scored a low total but we fought hard to put them into a difficult position, weathered it as they came back and then I got the opportunity to bowl the last over to seal it. It was a good day.'

In July 2009, Gordon captained Scotland for the first time in an Intercontinental Cup match against Canada, marking the occasion with an innings of 52, his highest first-class score. Although regular captain Gavin Hamilton then resumed his position, Gordon was appointed on a permanent basis in July the following year. He would lead Scotland to nine ODI victories and the finals of both the Intercontinental Cup and Division One of the World Cricket League in his twenty-one months at the helm.

'I prided myself on being a team man most of all,' he said. 'I took more joy out of a good team performance than anything I ever achieved as an individual. Beating Bangladesh in July 2012 for our first-ever win over a Full Member in a T20 International, for example, was hugely satisfying. Richie Berrington* was unbelievable for us that day.

'I remember him whacking a half-century against Ireland at The Grange as well, slog-sweeping Boyd Rankin for six before people did that sort of thing. A really gritty, nuggetty century from Qasim Sheikh against Ireland in the Intercontinental Cup sticks in my mind too. That was a terrific innings. It was a real privilege to be able to see performances like that from individuals who always stepped up for the team.'

Gordon's twenty-five ODI wickets came at an average of 37.28, with a best return of four for 41 against Canada in 2009. He took a further ninety-three in T20I, first-class and List A cricket to add to the 964 runs he scored for Scotland as a batsman across the four formats.

'All I tried to do was bowl my set and field as well as I could to make things as awkward as possible for the opposition,' he said. 'From my point of view, not being super-fast or very highly skilled meant that I had to have a strong mind-set to be able to make the most of what I did have as a cricketer. That I have that is down to the philosophy of my parents and the honest, working class atmosphere of Meigle.'

---

* Berrington's 58-ball hundred, the first in a T20I by an Associate cricketer, was only the seventh to have been scored in international cricket at that time.

In 2018, Gordon joined such luminaries as Leslie Balfour-Melville and James Aitchison in the Scottish Cricket Hall of Fame.

'At the age of twenty-three, if you'd told me where I'd be five years later, I would have thought that you were joking,' he said. 'But it just goes to show what can happen.'

*

Four years Gordon's junior, Annette followed the same initial path as her brother.

'I always played for Meigle as a youngster,' she said. 'I was the only girl, but it never seemed strange to me because it was just something I'd always done.

'It was only when I got to about thirteen or fourteen that it really struck me, I suppose. I had to get changed somewhere else which made me feel a bit different, and then the boys started bowling bouncers at me and it was: "Oh, hang on, they've suddenly gotten stronger and faster. This is a bit strange!"

'It was around that time that Clarence Parfitt saw me and suggested that I try out for Scotland. I met Kari [Carswell], and it was only then that I thought I might actually have a chance of achieving something I'd always dreamt of by playing for my country.'

After making her debut against Durham on 4 May 2002, Annette played in the International Women's Cricket Council Trophy, her first major international competition, in the Netherlands the following year. She finished the 2005 European Championships as Scotland's joint-highest run scorer, but as she took a break from the game to pursue her other sporting love, Annette suffered the first of the major injuries which have since blighted her career.

'When I was twenty-one I decided to concentrate on football,' she said. 'Pretty quickly, though, I tore my cruciate ligament so that was me, I couldn't do anything at all for a good couple of years.

'Cricket wasn't really on my mind as I was recovering, but I spent some time living out in Australia and that made me realise just how much I missed it. Wherever I looked people seemed to be playing, and I was desperate to go and join in with them. I went back to training, worked really hard and fell in love with it all over again.

'Cricket is like that. There can be a bit of a love-hate relationship with it at times – if you're in really bad form you just want to get as far away from it as possible!'

After returning to the Scotland side with a half-century against Northamptonshire in July 2013, Annette made a further thirty-seven appearances over the next three years to pass the milestone of fifty caps for her country.

'It was a real privilege,' she said. 'The opportunities I had to travel and play cricket in different parts of the world were amazing. We had a trip to China once to play in the Shanghai Sixes, which was great. There was a real sense of freedom about that competition. It gave us a chance to represent Scotland without the sense of pressure that we usually face, and that was really enjoyable.

'The Qualifier in Thailand was brilliant, too, because the girls did so well. For me personally it wasn't a great tournament, but for the team it was incredible. Like all of the family I pride myself on being a team player, and even if I can't contribute with the bat I know I can contribute to the team, which is just as important.

'And then the summer of 2016 was a huge highlight as well. Beating Holland so convincingly [in the Women's World Cup European Qualifier in Essex] was massive for us. Unfortunately, I broke my wrist shortly after that which put me out of contention for Sri Lanka. I've not had a lot of luck when it comes to injuries and that was a big disappointment.

'But a huge amount of credit goes to Kari. She worked so hard to change what had been a really negative mindset within the team in its early days.

'It's what we play for, after all. You don't go in to bat to be terrified of getting out, you go in to be positive. Seeing that change from being part of a team where we were all scared stiff to one that looked to take its chances and play good cricket in the process, was most exciting of all.'

*

While Peter Drummond represented his country at age-group level, too, fierce competition for the lone spot of wicketkeeper meant that his long-term career would remain in the club game.

'He is still one of the best wicketkeepers in Scotland,' said Gordon. 'To this day we have lads in the [Scotland] Under 19s who will come up to me to say that they have just played against him and how impressed they've been.

'In his younger days he used to pride himself on his stumpings, and that certainly helped me as a bowler as well. The amount of stumpings we used to get when we played together was unbelievable.'

But with three Strathmore and Perthshire Union Batting Aggregate Cups to his name as well as numerous awards at club level, it is as a batsman that Peter has had particular success.

'I have been an opener pretty much all the way through my career,' he said. 'I've always played much the same: fairly slow-scoring, nudged it around a bit, held an end up. The game has evolved a bit quicker than I have, you might say.'

'Peter would say that he is limited in certain areas, but that's fine,' said Gordon. 'Knowing that gives you more clarity in your game. He is one of those players with so much time, who knows his game inside-out and has that really dogged, competitive edge. His scoring record is phenomenal.'

'Technically Peter is an exceptional batsman,' agreed Annette. 'I think he is one of the most talented players not to have played for Scotland. He is probably the most competitive out of all of us, too. We all are, of course, but the rest of us maybe keep it a little bit more beneath the surface!'

Although a full international career was not to be, a move away from Meigle to nearby Forfarshire brought Peter experience of Scottish cricket at its highest domestic level.

'Gordon was living in Edinburgh and had been travelling back home to play, but when he decided to try and crack on at a higher level [with Watsonians] I thought that I should probably give it some thought as well,' he said. 'A few of us joined Forfarshire together, including [former Scotland captain] Ryan Watson, who had been

Meigle's professional for a while. Forfarshire had a lot of really good youngsters as well as a few older guys but they didn't have that many in the middle, so we kind of filled that hole for them. The first year we got promotion to the top division [of the Scottish National Cricket League] and stayed there for two years. It was good, serious cricket which I really enjoyed while I was there.'

The pull of home was strong, however, and at the beginning of 2009 Peter returned to Meigle, where he remains to this day.

'You never retire from playing for Meigle!' he laughed. 'But my biggest motivation these days is to do what I can to keep the club healthy. When you have your own personal goals and are achieving them it keeps you going, but now I'm looking at the kids coming through, their ambitions and their successes.

'They are the future of Meigle and that's my real inspiration today.'

And for Scottish cricket as a whole, what further inspiration might the future bring? The national side's progress in both men's and women's cricket has been matched by Cricket Scotland's off-field development, and for those at the heart of the organisation the ultimate goal is unequivocal.

'It is the short-term, mid-term and long-term ambition for Scottish cricket to become a Full Member of the ICC so our grass roots game can enjoy the benefits that brings,' Malcolm Cannon told *The Daily Telegraph*, two days before Scotland met England at The Grange. 'We will be ready very soon – in fact, it is probably more important when the ICC is ready. That is more likely to be the limiting factor. We will comply with the criteria reasonably soon, certainly within five years.'[1]

And so, after more than two and a half centuries, the next and most significant chapter in the story of cricket in Scotland is waiting to be written. Maybe, just maybe, that famous day in June 2018 was just a taste of things to come.

NOTES

Introduction: A Hidden Heritage
1. NL Stevenson: *'Play!'* (1946), p.13
2. Alex Massie: *Mike Denness and an All-Time Scottish Cricket XI*, *The Spectator*, 20 April 2013
3. David Potter: *The Encyclopaedia of Scottish Cricket* (1999), p.148
4. Richard S. Young: *As the Willow Vanishes* (2014), p.78
5. *The Spectator*, 20 April 2013

1. Twenty-Two of Kelso
1. *Kelso Chronicle*, 12 July 1850
2. *Gala Telegraph*, 19 August 1952

2. Carlton and the Champion
1. *Wisden Cricketers' Almanack* (1998), p.30
2. Sir Pelham Warner: *Lord's 1787-1945* (1946), pp.66-67
3. NL Stevenson: *'Play!'* (1946), p.15
4. From www.carltoncc.co.uk
5. *Edinburgh Evening Courant*, 12 June 1869
6. NL Stevenson: *'Play!'* (1946), p.20
7. Minutes of the meeting held at the Ship Hotel on 24 November 1871.
8. Robert H. Christie, quoted in NL Stevenson: *'Play!'* (1946), p.18
9. Ibid., p.20
10. Ibid.
11. Ibid.
12. DD Bone: *Fifty Years Reminiscences of Scottish Cricket* (1898), p.166
13. NL Stevenson: *'Play!'* (1946), p.20

14. Ibid.
15. Ibid.
16. DD Bone: *Fifty Years Reminiscences of Scottish Cricket* (1898), pp.148-150
17. Ibid., p.90
18. Ibid.
19. Quoted in NL Stevenson: *'Play!'* (1946), p.21

3. The Indomitable Carrick
1. Sir Pelham Warner: *Lord's 1787-1945* (1946), p.73
2. Tom Horan: *Felix on Bowling*, The Australasian, 2 October 1897
3. DD Bone: *Fifty Years Reminiscences of Scottish Cricket* (1898), p.133-135
4. Percival King (Ed.): *Scottish Cricketers' Annual* (1886), p.10
5. Ibid., p.11
6. *Cricket: A Weekly Record of the Game*, 24 September 1885
7. Percival King (Ed.): *Scottish Cricketers' Annual* (1886), p.12
8. Ibid.
9. NL Stevenson: *'Play!'* (1946), p.30
10. Percival King (Ed.): *Scottish Cricketers' Annual* (1886), p.14
11. DD Bone: *Fifty Years Reminiscences of Scottish Cricket* (1898), p.135

4. The Greatest Scot
1. *Cricket: A Weekly Record of the Game*, 7 June 1913
2. Ibid.
3. Ibid.
4. Grange scorebook, 1866-69 (courtesy of Neil Leitch)
5. *Cricket: A Weekly Record of the Game*, 7 June 1913
6. NL Stevenson: *'Play!'* (1946), p.80
7. Ibid., p.94
8. *Cricket: A Weekly Record of the Game*, 7 June 1913
9. Fraser Simm: *Saltire and Flannels* (2000)
10. Neil Leitch, *The Herald*, 13 March 2007
11. *The Scotsman*, 28 July 1882
12. *The Scotsman*, 30 July 1882
13. Ibid.
14. Ibid.
15. Ibid.
16. David Robson: 'New Light Shed on CB Fry: A Brilliant Cricketer, a Memorable Character', *ESPNcricinfo*, 20 September 1999

5. Shadows on the Esk
1. From www.mavisbank.org.uk
2. Percival King (Ed.): *Scottish Cricketers' Annual* (1888), p.1
3. Ibid.
4. John Thomson: *Drumpellier Cricket Club 1850-1906* (1906), p.115
5. Ibid.
6. Ibid.
7. DD Bone: *Fifty Years Reminiscences of Scottish Cricket* (1898), p.193

Bibliography

8. Ibid., p.204
9. JB Cairns: *Bright and Early* (1953), p.120
10. Ibid., p.119
11. Ibid., pp.119-120
12. Pencuik Cricket Club: *One Hundred Summers* (1946), p.18
13. Quoted in H.B. Tristram: *Loretto School* (1911), pp.241-242

6. Highland Games
1. *Dundee Courier*, 8 July 1869
2. *The Scotsman*, 7 September 1869
3. Memoir of John C. Campbell (unpublished), circa 1900.
4. Ibid.
5. *Dundee Evening Post*, 12 April 1905
6. *Dundee Evening Telegraph*, 5 October 1909
7. Ibid.

7. On the Promise of the Fruit
1. Alex Massie: 'The Keats of Cricket', *The Spectator*, 7 September 2009
2. David Frith: *Archie Jackson: The Keats of Cricket* (Revised Edition, 1987), p.xiii
3. Quoted in David Frith: *Archie Jackson: The Keats of Cricket* (Revised Edition, 1987), p.60
4. Ibid., p.62
5. David Frith: *Archie Jackson: The Keats of Cricket* (Revised Edition, 1987), p.63
6. *The Scotsman*, 17 July 1930
7. *The Scotsman*, 19 July 1930
8. *The Scotsman*, 20 July 1930
9. *The Scotsman*, 22 July 1930
10. Ibid.
11. Ibid.
12. Ibid.
13. Ibid.
14. Quoted in David Frith: *Archie Jackson: The Keats of Cricket* (Revised Edition, 1987), pp.68-69

8. The English Captain with a Scottish Heart
1. DR Jardine: *In Quest of the Ashes* (1933 – 2005 edition), p.164
2. Ibid., p.165
3. Ibid., p.164
4. Ibid.
5. David Hopps: *A Century of Great Cricket Quotes* (1998), p.213
6. Robert Philip: 'Jardine Family Keep the Faith', *The Daily Telegraph*, 1 December 2006
7. Quoted in David Frith: *Archie Jackson: The Keats of Cricket* (Revised Edition, 1987), p.100
8. DR Jardine: *In Quest of the Ashes* (2005 edition), p.241
9. Shane Warne: *No Spin* (2018), p.72
10. *The Guardian*, 20 June 1958

9. From the Ashes
1. From AK Bell's speech as he received the Freedom of the City of Perth in March 1938.
2. *Dundee Evening Post*, 27 July 1900
3. Ibid.
4. From www.espncricinfo.com
5. *Perthshire Advertiser*, 24 November 1934
6. Donald Bradman: *Farewell To Cricket* (1950), p.92

10. Memories of Manjrekar
1. *Wisden Cricketers' Almanack* (1984), p.1204
2. *Paisley Daily Express*, 3 May 1954
3. *Paisley Daily Express*, 14 July 1960
4. *Paisley Daily Express*, 28 June 1954
5. *Paisley Daily Express*, 13 September 1954

11. The History Boys
1. *Sydney Morning Herald*, 3 September 1985
2. Neil Drysdale: *Dad's Army* (2008 edition), p.69
3. *The Scotsman*, 2 September 1985
4. Tony Huskinson: 'Freuchie's Raiders Carry Off the Trophy', *The Cricketer International*, October 1985
5. Neil Drysdale: *Dad's Army* (2008 edition), p.149
6. Ibid., p.152
7. Ibid., p.153
8. Tony Huskinson: 'Freuchie's Raiders Carry Off the Trophy', *The Cricketer International*, October 1985
9. Neil Drysdale: *Dad's Army* (2008 edition), p.153
10. *The Scotsman*, 2 September 1985
11. Neil Drysdale: *Dad's Army* (2008 edition), p.156
12. Ibid.
13. Stephen McGinty: 'Scotland's Day but Botham Got the Whisky', *The Scotsman*, 6 September 2010

12. The Captain and the Goalie
1. Andy Goram (with Iain King): *The Goalie* (2009), p.136

13. Pushing the Boundaries
1. Isabelle Duncan: *Skirting the Boundary* (2013), pp. 107-108

14. The Generation Game
1. *The Daily Telegraph*, 8 June 2018

BIBLIOGRAPHY

The research behind this book would not have been possible without access to the vast online resources of CricketArchive, the Association of Cricket Statisticians and Historians, ESPNcricinfo and the British Newspaper Archive, all of which have been used extensively. I have also drawn on *Wisden Cricketers' Almanack*, Percival King's *Scottish Cricketers' Annual and Guide* and the early publication *Cricket: A Weekly Record of the Game*. In addition, the following books give further background and context to the stories I have covered and are most highly recommended.

DD Bone, *Fifty Years' Reminiscences of Scottish Cricket*, Aird & Coghill, 1898

Donald Bradman, *Farewell to Cricket*, Hodder and Stoughton, 1950

Gerald Brodribb, *Next Man In: A Survey of Cricket Laws and Customs*, Pelham Books, 1985

William Caffyn, *Seventy Not Out*, Public Domain, 1899

JB Cairns, *Bright and Early: A Bookseller's Memories of Edinburgh and Lasswade*, Cairns Brothers, 1953

Christopher Douglas, *Douglas Jardine: Spartan Cricketer*, George Allen & Unwin, 1984

Neil Drysdale, *Dad's Army: How Freuchie took Cricket by Storm*, The Parrswood Press, 2005

Isabelle Duncan, *Skirting the Boundary: A History of Women's Cricket*, The Robson Press, 2013

Jeremy Duncan, *A Roof Over One's Head: A Short History of the Gannochy Trust*, The Gannochy Trust, 2012

David Frith, *Archie Jackson: The Keats of Cricket*, Pavilion Books Limited, Revised Edition 1987

David Frith, *Bodyline Autopsy*, Aurum Press, 2002

Andy Goram (with Iain King), *The Goalie: My Story*, Mainstream Publishing Company, 2009

Duncan Hamilton, *Harold Larwood*, Quercus, 2009

David Hopps, *A Century of Great Cricket Quotes*, Robson Books Ltd., 1998

DR Jardine, *In Quest of the Ashes*, First published 1930, Methuen, 2005

Malcolm Knox, *Never a Gentleman's Game*, Hardie Grant, 2012

John Major, *More than a Game*, Harper Collins, 2007

Bibliography

Dr John A. Markland, *When AK met The Don*, The Gannochy Trust, 2012

Penicuik Cricket Club, *One Hundred Summers 1844-1944*, Pillans and Wilson, 1946

David W. Potter, *The Encyclopaedia of Scottish Cricket*, Empire Publications Ltd., 1999

David W. Potter, *The Western Union 1893-1997*, David Potter, 2013

David W. Potter, *Cricket in the East*, David Potter, 2014

Scott Reeves, *The Champion Band*, Chequered Flag Publishing, 2014

Peter M. Reid, *Ferguslie Cricket Club 1887-1987*, Ferguslie CC, 1987

Fraser Simm, *Saltire and Flannels*, Fraser Simm, 2000

NL Stevenson, *'Play!': The Story of Carlton Cricket Club and a Personal Record of Over 50 Years' Scottish Cricket*, CJ Cousland & Sons, 1946

John Thomson, *Drumpellier Cricket Club 1850-1906*, Baird and Hamilton, 1906

Richard Tomlinson, *Amazing Grace: The Man who was WG*, Little Brown, 2015

HB Tristram, *Loretto School*, T. Fisher Unwin, 1911

Sir Pelham Warner, *Lord's 1787-1945*, Harrap and Co, 1946

Tim Wigmore and Peter Miller, *Second XI: Cricket in its Outposts*, Pitch Publishing, 2015

Richard S. Young, *As the Willow Vanishes: Glasgow's Forgotten Legacy*, Consilience Media, 2014

Acknowledgements

The Secret Game would not have been written were it not for Donald MacLeod, Chief Photographer at Cricket Scotland. It was at his suggestion that we collaborated on the short series of illustrated articles in 2017 which marked the beginning of my research into the history of the Scottish club game, and it is entirely down to his inspiration that the concept for this book was developed. Donald's knowledge of the Scottish scene and eye for a 'hook' is second to none, and his experience, guidance and, not least, sense of humour has been very much appreciated. I am proud to share the Raeburn Place press box with him still.

I am enormously indebted to Cricket Scotland historian Neil Leitch as well as Stuart Black, Mark Bridgeman and Richard 'Siggy' Young, each of whom offered me access to their respective archives as well as much time, advice and kindness. Their contribution has been enormously valuable, and Siggy's masterful book, *As the Willow*

Acknowledgements

Vanishes, has been an inspiration. My heartfelt gratitude also goes to Cameron Munro and David M. Potter for their additional assistance in filling in the blanks I often encountered, and to Scott Reeves of Chequered Flag Publishing for his much-appreciated support.

I would like to thank Abbi Aitken-Drummond, Annette Aitken-Drummond, Ramsay Allan, Chris Anderson, David Armstrong, Robbie Birrell, John Boyd, Robin Bradley-Roake, Neil Cameron, Malcolm Cannon, Kari Carswell, Dave Christie, John Downie, Gordon Drummond, Peter J. Drummond, Peter CJ Drummond, Graham Ferguson, Ben Fox, Stephen Green, David Harrowes, Ian Henderson, Iona Jardine, Iain Kennedy, Jack Kennedy, Brian Lang, Iain Leggat, Graeme Leslie, John McCabe, Gordon McKinnie, Paul Macari, John Markland, Sandy Mathieson, Misbah-ul-Haq, George Pollock, Moghees Sheikh, Lizzie Sleet, Kris Steel, Stephen Thompson, Craig White, Kathryn White and Michael Yan Hip. Their insight has been invaluable and their time very much appreciated. The Scottish cricket community is truly generous.

Thank you, too, to the Gannochy Trust, the International Cricketers Association and the Mavisbank Trust as well as, of course, Cricket Scotland.

Finally, my special thanks go to Susan, Emma and Douglas for their infinite patience as I spend each summer either standing on a cricket field or sitting with a laptop at the edge of one. This is for them.

Index

a'Beckett, Ted 78
Adams, Jimmy 131
Aitchison, James 111-112, 163
Aitken-Drummond, Abbi 146-147, 149, 151-153
Aitken-Drummond, Annette 153, 157-159, 163-164, 166
Albion CC 5
Alexander, Gilbert 76
Ali, Azhar 6
All-England Eleven 12-14, 16, 18, 20-21, 36, 45
Almond Valley CC 101-102
Anderson, George 20
Anderson, Tom 41
Annandale, JH 54
Arbuthnot, G 54
Asher, Augustus 56, 58
Aslam, Sahar 151

Balfour-Melville, Leslie 44-51, 56, 163
Ballinluig CC 64-65, 68
Balmain District CC 73-74, 79
Bannerman, Alick 37, 49
Bannerman, Charles 37
Bannerman, Edward 48
Baxter, Sandy 78
Beal, Charles 49
Bell, Arthur Kinmond 92-97, 100, 103-105
Berrington, Richie 162
Berwick CC 10-11, 55
Birnam CC 63

Black, Stuart 106, 115
Blain, John 161
Bodyline 80, 82-83, 85-89, 96
Border League 10, 134
Botham, Ian 4, 122-123
Boyle, Harry 50
Bradman, Don 5, 23, 72, 74-75, 77-80, 86, 89, 95-100, 104
Brampton, Charles 17
Brannan, Pete 135
Breadalbane CC 62, 64-71, 91, 118
Brown, David 49
Brunt, Katherine 145
Bryce, Kathryn 153
Bryce, Sarah 153
Buchanan, James 57-58

Caffyn, William 14, 17-18
Caldwell, Alfred 13-14, 49, 57, 59
Caldwell, Gordon 60
Caldwell, Herbert 57
Caledonian CC 31-32, 39
Campbell, Archibald 41
Campbell, Gavin 64
Campbell, John C 65, 67
Campbell, Tom 6
Cannon, Malcolm 3, 167
Cardus, Neville 91
Carlton CC 2, 7, 22, 25-28, 31, 55, 111
Carlton Ground, Edinburgh 26
Carrick-Buchanan, DCR 20, 36
Carrick, John 40-41
Carrick, J. Stewart 35-36, 39, 40-44

Index

Carswell, Kari (née Anderson) 140-154, 163, 165
Chalmers, George 69
Chalmers, Tom 38-39, 48
Charlwood, Henry 22, 29-31
Chichester Priory Park CC 35, 38, 43, 70
Christie, Brian 121
Christie, Dave 117, 121-122
Clarke, William 12-16, 18, 21
Clutha CC 36
Clydesdale CC 9, 31, 58, 114
Constantine, Learie 87
Cotterill, Joseph 27, 29-31, 50
County Championship 185
Cowan, David 118-120
Cowan, Ed 160
Cowan, Lily 59
Craig, John 41, 49
Craigmount Park, Edinburgh 26-27, 29-30, 41
Crichton, Andy 120
Crichton, David 58
Crichton, George 121
Cricket Scotland 2-3, 102, 108, 131, 144, 147-148, 154, 159, 167
Currie, Donald 66

Daft, Richard 19, 23
Dall House 66-68
Dean, James 'Jemmy' 16
Denness, Mike 6
Dickins, George 19-20
Diver, Alfred 14
Don Wauchope, Andrew 56
Doo'cot Park, Perth 95, 97, 99-101, 103
Downie, John 131-133, 135
Drake, Edward 17
Drummond, Gordon 157, 159-162, 165-166
Drummond, Peter CJ 157, 159
Drummond, Peter J 157, 165-167
Drummond, Peter M 157-158
Drumpellier CC 36, 46, 55-58, 69, 112-113
Duncan, Alan 120
Duncan, Alexander 29

Dunkeld CC 63
Dunlop CC 118
Dupplin, Viscount 14

Edinburgh Academicals CC 45-46, 50, 55-56, 126, 135
Edinburgh Caledonian CC 26
Emmett, Tom 45

Falkland CC 130
Ferguslie CC 105-115
Fingleton, Jack 88-89
Forfarshire CC 5, 93
Free Foresters CC 45
Freuchie CC 116-124

Gala CC 93
Galashiels CC 10, 55
Garrett, Tom 49
Gentlemen of Scotland 45
Gilchrist, Adam 6, 105
Glamis Castle 47
Glasgow Academicals CC 39, 102
Glasgow Green 5
Goram, Andy 130-134
Gordon, Kirstie 7, 152-153
Grace, Fred 28-30, 33
Grace, WG 23-24, 26, 28-31, 33, 35, 37, 41-42, 45, 51, 56
Grange CC 30, 45, 55-56, 78, 94, 111
Greenidge, Gordon 6
Greenock CC 107, 113-114
Green, Stephen 136
Gregory, Dave 36
Grierson, M 59
Griffith, George 19
Grimmett, Clarrie 76
Grundy, James 17-18

Haggo, Samantha 153
Hamilton Crescent, Glasgow 36-37, 43, 77, 95, 126, 132
Hamilton, Gavin 161
Hammond, Walter 75
Hawick and Wilton CC 10
Hayman, CH 27
Haynes, Desmond 6

Henderson, Tommy 117
Hillhead CC 134
Holder, Adzil 115
Holyrood Park, Glasgow 31
Horan, Tom 38
Hornibrook, Percy 76
Hughes, Kim 6
Humphrey, Richard 28
Hunt, Bill 79
Huntly CC 7
Hussey, Michael 108

Inzamam-ul-Haq 126
Irvine, Stewart 120
Ivanhoe CC 65
I Zingari CC 46

Jack, Lorna 153
Jackson, Archie 6, 72-81, 88
Jardine, Douglas 81-91, 96
Jardine, Fianach 84-85, 87-91
Jemmy Dean 19-20
Jones, Sammy 49
Jupp, Harry 22, 28-29, 31

Kanhai, Rohan 6
Kasperek, Leigh 7, 148
Kelburne CC 109, 114, 126
Kelso CC 8-12, 14-21, 26, 55, 58, 130
Kennedy, Iain 109-110, 115
Kennedy, Jack 107
Kerr, John 76
Kilmarnock CC 111, 114
Kippax, Alan 78
Kirkhill, Penicuik 127, 130-131, 136
Kirkhope, Ian 130
Knox, Steve 153

Laidlay, William 30
Langer, Justin 6, 105
Larwood, Harold 74-75, 79-81, 87, 96
Lasswade CC 53-62, 69
Latif, Rashid 126
Leslie, Graham 128, 130-131, 134
Lillywhite, James 9, 18, 21-22, 27, 30, 33, 35, 40-41, 43, 57
Lillywhite, John 9, 17, 23

Lockyer, Tom 17-18

MacKellar, Craig 126
Macnair, Robert 49
Malhotra, Ashok 108
Manderston CC 10
Manjrekar, Vijay 105-109, 112-115
Mannes, Charles 69
Mannofield, Aberdeen 5
Manou, Graham 126
Maqsood, Abtaha 153
Martin, Chris 6
Martindale, Manny 87
Marylebone CC (MCC) 14, 16-17, 24, 36-38, 46, 57, 60, 67-68, 86-88, 90-91, 96, 98
Mathieson, Sandy 106, 115
Mavisbank House 52-55, 57-58, 60-61, 69
Mayfield CC 101-102
McAllister, Andrew 31
McCabe, Stan 80, 88
McDonald, Duncan 27
McGill, Katie 153
McGregor, Angus 69
McInnes, Charles 31
McNaughton, Niven 119-121, 123
McNeill, John 36
McTavish, Alastair 76
Meigle CC 117-118, 156-159, 162-163, 166-167
Meikleriggs, Paisley 106, 108, 111, 113-115
Melrose CC 10
Misbah-ul-Haq 127-130, 135-137
Mortlock, William 20
Morton, Willie 130
Mudie, William 20
Murdoch, Billy 37, 48-50

National Village Championship 116-119, 123
Nel, Dewald 161
New Williamfield, Stirling 139
Noble, Monty 70
Northern CC 101-102
North Inch, Perth 5, 93, 100

INDEX

Oldfield, Bert 80
Orr, Jimmy 109-110, 112-115

Paget, Henry 14
Palmer, Eugene 49
Pandit, Balan 108, 115
Parfitt, Clarence 144, 163
Parr, George 18, 45
Peacock, Matt 113
Penicuik CC 53, 55, 59, 102, 125-137
Perth Doo'cot CC 102-103
Perthshire CC 5, 93, 100, 102
Pitlochry CC 63, 65
Ponsford, Bill 80
Pooley, Ted 30-31
Priddle, Liz 153
Priory Park, Chichester 35, 38, 40, 42-43, 70

Qadir, Abdul 6
Queen's Park FC 9, 39

Raeburn Place, Edinburgh 34, 39, 45-46, 48, 76, 83
Rae, Ollie 153
Rajput, Lal 105
Ranken, RB 45
Rayner, GF 27
Raza, Sikandar 6
Renny-Tailyour, Henry 48
Reynolds, Frederick 20
Richardson, JB 27-28, 30
Richardson, Vic 80
Rizwan-uz-Zaman 128
Rossie Priory CC 118
Rowledge CC 119-121
Royal High Corstorphine CC 126, 134-135
Royal High School CC 55, 131

Sagar, Scott 130
Sanderson, Henry 59
Scarlett, Reg 108
Scholes, Rachel 153
Scottish County Championship 93
Scottish Cricket Union 25, 36, 50, 77, 83, 108
Scottish National League 10
Scott, Robert 57
Selkirk CC 9, 10, 55
Shacklock, Frank 57-58
Shaw, James 45
Shedden Park, Kelso 10, 12, 14, 17, 20-21
Sheikh, Qasim 162
Snowball, Betty 139
Somerville, WA 54, 56-58, 60
Soutar, James 69
Southerton, James 22, 27, 30-31, 33
Spark's Ground, Edinburgh 13, 45
Spence, Linda 142, 144-145
Spofforth, Fred 37-38, 46, 79
St Boswells CC 117
St Clair Grant, William 28
Steel, Kris 135-136
Stevenson, Norman 2
Stewart's Melville Royal High CC 126, 134
Stirling County CC 127, 139-141
St Leonards School 139
Strathearn CC 101-102

Tennant, Andy 147
Thistle CC 5
Thompson, Peter 49
Thomson, ADR 32, 40, 55-56, 58, 136
Thomson, Lawrence 32
Thomson, Stephen 136
Tinley, Francis 14-15
Tod, Ben 78
Trewartha, Terry 118, 120-121

Uddingston CC 109, 113, 126, 130, 133
United All-England Eleven 16, 18, 20
United South of England Eleven 22-23, 26, 28-32, 34, 39, 41
Urquhart, Fiona 151, 153

Vernon-Wentworth, Bruce 66-67
Voce, Bill 75

Warner, Pelham 24, 38

West Lothian CC 129-130
West of Scotland CC 20, 31, 35-37, 39,
        41, 43, 55, 69, 110-111, 114
White, Kathryn 141-142, 145-146, 153
Wilkie, Mark 120
Wilson, George 120, 123-124
Wisden, John 16, 18
Wolfhill CC 94
Wood, Alfred 49
Woodfull, Bill 75, 80
Wood, WL 70
Wright, Craig 161

Yan Hip, Michael 128, 130, 132, 134

ALSO FROM CHEQUERED FLAG PUBLISHING

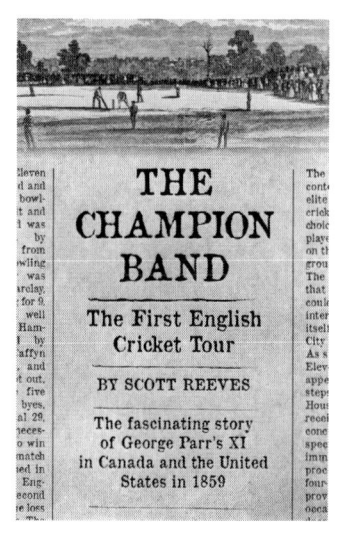

THE CHAMPION BAND

The First English Cricket Tour

by Scott Reeves

CRICKET WEB BEST NEW WRITER 2015
LONGLISTED CRICKET SOCIETY & MCC BOOK OF THE YEAR 2015

In 1859, twelve cricketers left Liverpool to embark on the first overseas tour by a representative England side. Their destination was the place where cricket looked most likely to flourish: Canada and the United States.

It was not an easy trip - the English players experienced death on the high seas, were threatened at gunpoint and sensed unrest in the pre-Civil War USA.

Led by George Parr, the English tourists came up against the best of the New World cricketers. Some of the locals would go on to pioneer the sport that ultimately caused the death of North American cricket: baseball.

A gripping account featuring original research, THE CHAMPION BAND tells the fascinating story of the first English cricket tour.

HOWZAT FOR A GREAT CRICKET BOOK?

Chequered Flag
PUBLISHING

WWW.CHEQUEREDFLAGPUBLISHING.CO.UK